Profitability and Law Firm Management

Other titles available from Law Society Publishing:

E-Business Basics for Law Firms (due 2003)
Christina Archbold
1 85328 752 0

Excellent Client Service (due 2003)
Heather Stewart
1 85328 777 6

The Internet: Business Strategies for Law Firms
Andrew Terrett
1 85328 582 X

Lexcel Office Procedures Manual
Matthew Moore and Michael Dodd
1 85328 710 5 (includes disk)

Lexcel Assessment Guide
The Law Society
1 85328 705 9

Managing Cyber-Risks
Rupert Kendrick
1 85328 771 7

Marketing, Management and Motivation
Dianne Bown-Wilson and Gail Courtney
1 85328 810 1

Marketing Your Law Firm
Lucy Adam
1 85328 745 8 (includes CD-Rom)

Quality Management for Law Firms
Matthew Moore
1 85328 715 6

Setting Up and Managing a Small Practice (2nd edition)
Martin Smith
1 85328 792 X

Solicitors and Financial Services (3rd edition)
Peter Camp
1 85328 805 5

Solicitors' Guide to Good Management (2nd edition)
Trevor Boutall and Bill Blackburn
1 85328 732 6

All books from Law Society Publishing can be ordered through good bookshops or direct from our distributors, Marston Book Services, by telephone 01235 465656 or e-mail law.society@marston.co.uk. Please confirm the price before ordering.

For further information or a catalogue, please telephone our editorial and marketing office on 020 7320 5878.

Profitability and Law Firm Management

Andrew Otterburn

The Law Society

ISBN 1 85328 820 9

Published in 2002 by the Law Society
113 Chancery Lane, London WC2A 1PL

Typeset by J&L Composition, Filey, North Yorkshire
Printed by TJ International Ltd, Padstow, Cornwall

To
Debbie, Joanna and Samuel

Contents

About the author

Andrew Otterburn is a chartered accountant and management consultant, and has been advising solicitors since 1989.

He was Grant Thornton's senior legal consultant for a number of years before setting up his own firm in 1996. He now works from home in West Yorkshire and has two colleagues, Dr Heather Stewart and Kevin Butler, who are based in Ilkley and London respectively.

Since 1989 he has advised around 150 firms of solicitors within the UK, mainly in connection with the management of their firms and future strategy. Clients range from sole principals to larger firms with around 50 partners and extend from the north east of Scotland to the south coast of England. They include firms in Edinburgh, London, northern England, East Anglia and the South West. In addition to consultancy work he undertakes a large number of seminars each year on behalf of the Law Society and other professional bodies, and runs an annual Management Forum at Le Manoir Aux Quat' Saisons in Oxfordshire.

Preface

Developments since 1998

During 1997 and the first half of 1998, I had the pleasure of writing two books on behalf of the Law Society: *Profitability and Financial Management*, which was published in the spring of 1998, and *Cashflow and Improved Financial Management*, which was published a few months later. The latter was distributed free of charge to firms with 10 and fewer partners by the Law Society.

This new volume updates both books and seeks to move them forward. Professional life has continued to become more complicated and the need for firms to have clear, simple and focused management is more important than ever. Whilst primarily focused on financial management, this book once again starts, and ends, by considering the wider management issues facing firms, because successful financial management does not happen in isolation. It is part of the wider management of a firm of solicitors.

Since 1998 the Law Society has made considerable progress in the help it provides firms in relation to practice management. In particular, the Law Management Section[1] was launched in 1998. By autumn 2002 it had approximately 1,500 members and now undertakes an annual financial benchmarking survey sponsored by accountants BDO Stoy Hayward. This survey includes useful benchmarks of performance, and a number of them from the 2001 survey are included in this book.

In 1999 the Law Society also launched its Lexcel[2] quality accreditation scheme and by autumn 2002 more than 250 practices were accredited. Many of these firms have seen their practice management improve as a direct result of implementing the necessary procedures. If you are not familiar with Lexcel, a copy of the standard is included in Appendix A and on the disk[3] that accompanies this book. The disk also contains a copy of the Lexcel Self-Assessment Checklist (included at Appendix B).

Over the past four years the Law Society of Scotland has also started publishing an annual survey of law firms in Scotland, and, for the benefit of readers in Scotland, this book includes a number of financial benchmarks from the 2001 survey.[4]

About this book

This volume is divided into three parts:

- Part I – The prerequisites of good financial management: Overall practice management;
- Part II – Understanding the figures;
- Part III – Improving long-term profitability.

This book is not intended to be the definitive or only way of doing things, but is designed to help partners and others involved in practice management think about their firms and identify ways of making them more successful. Its purpose is to help you move forward.

As in the previous titles, this book tries to avoid simply suggesting what you should do, but shows you how to do it, and the attached disk once again includes a number of example formats – this time in Microsoft Word and Excel – for you to use and modify as appropriate.

Andrew Otterburn
Holmfirth
October 2002

Notes

1   Law Management Section: for details telephone 020 7316 5736 or e-mail marga.auz@lawsociety.org.uk
2   Lexcel: for details telephone 020 7320 5769 or e-mail paula.crowhurst@lawsociety.org.uk
3   Word documents on disk: Lexcel Practice Management Standard and Lexcel Self-Assessment Questionnaire.
4   The 2001 Survey of Law Firms in Scotland: for details telephone 0131 476 8164 or e-mail lisaanderson@lawscot.org.uk

Acknowledgements

I should like to thank the many people who have contributed quotes and comments for inclusion in this book.

My thanks to Julia Snow, partner with Barnett Sampson in London, for her continuing support and encouragement.

I should also like to acknowledge the work of the many Law Society staff I have worked with in recent years – some of whom are no longer with the Society – for the contribution and initiative they have shown in helping firms improve the management of their practices. These are the people who often come up with the good ideas and work hard to see them through. In particular, John Miller, Gail Hardcastle, Mitzi Wyman, Christina Archbold, Maureen Miller, Matt Duggan, Marga Auz, Gerald Newman, Tracey Stanley, Ian Croft, Tim Toghill and Morag Goldfinch.

I should like to thank James Boyd, Director of Finance at Cobbetts in Manchester and Leeds, and David Auty, Finance Director of Walker Morris in Leeds, for their contributions and ideas whilst I was writing this book.

I should also like to thank: Maureen Miller of the Law Society, and Mark Green and Nick Carter-Pegg of BDO Stoy Hayward for allowing me to use charts from the Law Management Section Financial Benchmarking Survey 2001; Bruce Ritchie of the Law Society of Scotland for allowing me to use charts from the 2001 Survey of Law Firms in Scotland.

The prerequisites of good financial management: Overall practice management

Managing a law firm

A model for success

In an article published in summer 2001,[1] James Dallas, Chairman of Denton Wilde Sapte, described the four key elements for success in a law firm as:

- being clear about our chosen area of business;
- finding and keeping good people;
- delivering an excellent service to clients;
- securing a financial return that enables us to reward our people and invest in the continuing development of the business.

These four elements hold true regardless of the size or location of your firm, and are as applicable to an inner city legal aid practice as they are to a major commercial firm. They do not just happen, however, on their own. Firms have to work hard, over a long period of time, to achieve these four elements.

In particular, success nowadays is rarely just down to having technically good lawyers – although that does help! Having people with the technical skills appropriate for the type of work you do, who are motivated and who work hard is an important starting point, but is no longer sufficient to guarantee success, as many partners in high street firms will testify. Success today has as much to do with the way your firm is run and structured, your sense of where it and the markets you serve are going, and your ability to lead and motivate others, especially your fellow partners.

The problem is that many find the 'management' of their firm a difficult area and one they feel they do not have the training to tackle. The truth is, of course, that good management is not complicated and good managers often know instinctively how to respond. They know this because they have good people skills, good instincts – and courage. Those of us not born with these skills – and that is most of us – can often learn many of them, and in particular can learn to recognise our own limitations and begin to better appreciate the strengths of others.

Management should therefore be as uncomplicated as possible, and your objective should be to devise a solution that is simple, that is appropriate for your firm, and that draws on the strengths and talents of the people you have – partners and staff. In particular, don't lose sight of what your staff can contribute, because you don't have to be an equity partner in order to have ideas and to be able to play a role in the management and development of a firm.

The problems of 'management' in a law firm

Management is relatively easy in large law firms. If you have 20 or 30 partners, everyone accepts there is a need for effective and professional management, and the partners recognise that they can afford for some of their colleagues to do little or no fee earning. Sometimes the acid test is when you can no longer all easily sit around the partners' table – it becomes obvious that the firm needs to be run in a different way.

At this size of firm there will generally be non-lawyer managers – professionals in areas such as finance, information technology (IT), marketing and human resources (HR) – brought in to make the whole management of the firm more effective. Partners will still be involved, but their roles will be different.

Management is also relatively straightforward in very small firms. If there are just two partners, perhaps one other fee earner, and three or four staff, management often happens instinctively. You will all work closely together, everyone will know what is going on, and your main concerns are likely to be the demands of your clients – and a lack of time. This time pressure is likely to be compounded by much of the administration of the firm, especially staff issues, falling on the shoulders of the partners – or typically one particular partner. At this size of firm there will be a cashier, and he or she will be a key person, upon whose shoulders much of the firm's administration will fall. These people are often key to day-to-day administration.

The main problem is frequently in mid-sized firms – those with between five and 15 partners, of whom there are a large number in England and Wales. At this size of firm the partners are very often the principal fee earners and management will invariably take second place to fee earning. Often in firms of this size there will be two or three partners who recognise the need to run their firm differently; however, most will not be particularly interested. In many cases, these partners will happily let someone else worry about the management of the firm, leaving them free to concentrate on client work. In other cases they will interfere and undermine.

In this size of firm the role of partners is often blurred – they are part fee earner, part manager, part owner. The transition from a small firm, where all the partners are involved in most decisions, to a style that is more 'corporate' is difficult, and can be very evident. Generally there will be a practice manager, but the role can be problematic if it has not been properly thought through. Also, because of a desire to keep the administrative salaries bill under control, these people tend to be overloaded and are forced to take on too much.

Management in these mid-sized firms is typically undertaken by partners who also have high workloads. The areas in which they often have special difficulty include:

- a lack of time;
- striking a balance between management and fee earning;
- getting their partners to accept innovation and change;
- getting their partners to work together as a team;
- communications;
- achieving a reasonable level of profitability.

In spring 2002 these difficulties were illustrated by the responses from partners at seminars in Cambridge, Manchester and Norwich. Delegates from around 45 mainly small and medium-sized firms were asked to complete a one-page questionnaire, scoring their own firm in respect of 10 areas (see Table 1.1). The table highlights some of the areas in which firms often have difficulties and those that are easier to tackle.

The participants scored themselves surprisingly well on their sense of a clear vision of where their firm is going – an area firms generally find difficult. They had greater difficulty actually planning for the future – something many partners will relate to.

Many would also identify with the difficulty of getting people to change and most managing partners would readily agree that it is easier to get their staff to change than their fellow partners! Most participants felt their partners worked well as a team – although there was a broad spread on this question with many (especially smaller firms) scoring themselves well, but 10 per cent of participants scoring themselves poorly.

Most of the firms were reasonably happy with their management structures although a number felt they were not making good use of professional managers – practice managers, and HR, finance and marketing professionals.

Although some participants rated themselves highly on their ability to challenge working methods, most scored themselves only 'good' on this area. Changing working methods, especially the full utilisation of IT, is generally a sphere in which many firms are weak.

Communication was highlighted as a difficult area for many firms – both vertically between partners/team leaders and staff, but especially horizontally, across departments. Communication is invariably difficult and is often most difficult in firms that are highly departmentalised. For firms in more than one town, or with more than one office, or on different floors, communication becomes even more demanding. The first casualty of poor communications between departments or teams is cross-selling, so it is important this area is dealt with.

Table 1.1 Number of partner responses to questionnaire

Please score your firm against the following criteria (on a scale from 7 [Excellent] to 1 [Poor])	Excellent		Good		OK		Poor
	7	6	5	4	3	2	1
Our sense of a clear vision of where our firm is going and a focus on the markets we wish to serve	3	10	18	8	4	–	1
Our ability to plan for the future	3	4	17	10	6	1	3
The receptiveness of my partners to innovation and change	2	6	11	8	12	1	1
The receptiveness of our staff to innovation and change	1	6	19	9	7	1	–
The degree to which my partners work together as a team	2	9	10	10	7	2	2
The strength of our management structure	2	14	8	11	5	1	1
Our use of professional managers	3	5	14	3	7	4	3
Our ability to challenge working methods and the way work is processed	2	4	14	10	7	6	–
Communications between partners, team leaders and staff	1	6	13	6	10	6	–
Communications between departments	–	1	12	8	9	7	3
Our ability to develop our people and use their strengths to the full	–	7	12	14	10	1	–

The questionnaire showed a wide spread in firms' abilities to get the most out of their people, and this is true for firms generally. Only a minority of firms are very good at developing their people and building on their strengths. People development, and areas such as appraisals, are probably one of the hardest things for many practices to get right. They will have an appraisal system – it is a requirement of both Lexcel and the Legal Services Commission's Specialist Quality Mark (SQM) – but in reality many will just pay lip service to the idea. This is often because they have had no training, but can also be because the partners simply do not understand how such techniques can be used to make their practices more successful.

You might like to score your own firm against each of these criteria and ask your partners to do the same – it can be interesting to see if you all perceive the problem in the same way! There is a copy of the questionnaire on the disk accompanying this book.[2]

Larger firms, with more than 20 partners, will often score themselves better on many of the above criteria. Their main problem areas are also often focused on their partners, specifically their receptiveness to change and the degree to which they work as a team.

The concept of 'management' as opposed to 'administration'

Part of the problem of management is often caused by confusion about what we actually mean by 'management', and the distinction between 'management' and 'administration'.

Equity partners in most firms typically work a 10–12 hour day although it is not uncommon for only six or seven of those hours to be chargeable time. Those with specific management responsibilities may achieve only three or four chargeable hours a day. A considerable amount of partner time is therefore spent on non-chargeable work.

In many cases the partners will be using their non-chargeable time in an effective way. They may be supervising more junior staff, they may be involved in marketing, or other valuable non-chargeable work. In other instances, however, partners will confuse management with administration and get involved with things that have to be done, but not necessarily by them. Examples include:

- changing the paper in the photocopier – described by more than one managing partner as enjoyable, because it gave them a break from fee earning;
- dealing with temporary secretaries;
- being IT 'supremo' – the person the secretaries go to when their printers are not working;
- fixing minor staff problems;
- being on reception and taking responsibility for office juniors;
- being the legal aid franchise representative;
- dealing with PAYE and VAT returns.

It is highly debatable whether partners should be undertaking these types of role, whether they are going to do them well, and whether this represents a good use of their time. If you assume a partner chargeout rate of £100 an hour, two or three hours a day soon mounts up to a significant annual amount – approaching £60,000, and more than sufficient to pay the salary of a good practice manager.

Whilst a partner might need to take overall responsibility for administration they rarely need to do it themselves. Partner input to management should be at team level, or strategic level for the firm as a whole.

If you are involved in the management of your firm:

- try listing all of the 'management' tasks you do for a week (and note how long each took);
- at the end of the week add up the total – how much time you spent on 'management' – and be prepared to be shocked. Then go through the list and critically ask, in respect of each item, was it 'management' or administration? Were you the correct person to do it? If not who should have done it?

You may well have decided, by the time you have finished this exercise, that you should not be doing quite a number of the items on the list. You may also have decided you can justify the recruitment of a practice or office manager, or to move an existing member of staff into that position. This may increase the firm's payroll, but hopefully it will increase its fee-earning capacity by at least the same amount. You may also have reduced your own stress levels, and at the very least may be feeling more positive!

Time is the one thing most partners lack, and it must be used carefully. Partner input into management should be more concerned with strategic issues and with driving the business forward. The starting point will be your firm's management structure and your role in the management of the business, and time devoted to that role should not be undervalued. It is as important as fee earning and, many would argue, more so. Partner time spent with other members of your team, or with other members of staff is time well spent. The problem is that pressures on time can result in partners simply undertaking their fee-earning work and paying lip service to management. Because of these pressures it is sometimes necessary to discipline oneself to make time for management.

In the case study below, a managing partner of a six-partner Merseyside firm explains how she uses 'Management By Walking About' to make sure she sees her staff.

In essence, the issue is to review your firm's management, and its operation, to distinguish between management and administration, and to decide who should actually do what.

CASE STUDY **Managing partner**

It is very easy for everyone to be isolated because of the geography of the building. I have to be sure I have different routes for routine tasks that take me to most places as a matter of course just so I can be seen. Some people may think I am at the top of the building to hide away so I need to get around and be seen. It is amazing how much I learn each time! It is also good exercise, especially for those practising in old Georgian buildings with no lifts! The last time I counted, the accounts department housed in the basement and I were 66 stairs apart. But it is the only exercise I get during the week! By making sure I meet and talk to my staff I know what is going on and they can update me daily, hourly, on the things I need to know.

A five-stage approach

It is very useful periodically – perhaps every three to five years – to review your firm's structure. The main stages in this, and in improving a firm's management and long-term profitability, are:

1. To critically assess its operational structure.
2. To establish a management structure appropriate to this operational structure, to define the various roles, and to identify the best people to fill these roles.
3. For these people to lead the preparation of business and marketing plans, and budgets, for each team or business unit.
4. To translate these team plans into individual objectives and an action plan for each fee earner and member of staff.
5. To introduce effective financial management controls and establish a simple reporting system so that progress can be monitored and the plans modified and revised on an ongoing basis.

The last three of these items are dealt with later in this book. The first two are discussed below.

Operational structure

By 'operational structure' I mean the actual organisation of your fee earners into teams, departments and offices.

A firm's operational structure is an important starting point when considering an appropriate management structure and when reviewing your business as a whole. How you are organised on the ground has a big impact on the type and nature of management structure required to steer your firm forward. There is a big difference, for example, between on the one hand a single-office firm occupying one floor on an open plan basis and on the other a multi-office firm.

Traditionally firms have often been organised on an office basis, with accounts prepared for each office and fee earners in an office reporting to a partner in that office. Although this has some practical advantages, it can result in the true strength of a firm not being realised and in fee earners being isolated from others doing the same work. Figure 1.1 illustrates a firm organised on an office basis, with a partner in charge of each office. Most areas of law are offered from all the offices, but the fee earners in each team are geographically spread and some of the work types have just one fee earner in an office.

The main problems with the type of operating structure illustrated are that fee earners become isolated from colleagues doing similar work, it can be difficult to develop true expertise and depth of experience, and the overall strength of a firm in a particular area of work can be understated. This method of working can also cause problems with cover during holidays and a lack of technical back-up and supervision.

Office-based structure

Fee earners	Office 1	Office 2	Office 3	Office 4	Total
Conveyancing	2	2	1	1	6
Personal injury	2	1	1	1	5
Family	1	3	1	1	6
Trust and Probate	1	1	1	1	4
Crime	1	1	2	3	7
Commercial	2	0	0		2
Total	9	8	6	7	30

Team-based structure

Figure 1.1   Operational structure, office-based

One multi-office firm with this structure had quite a large family department, with eight fee earners, but it was only when they met as a team and prepared a team business and marketing plan for the family team as a whole that their true strength became apparent.

Simply reviewing how your firm operates can be a very useful starting point in reassessing your business. The key is to sit back and take an objective view, and be prepared at least to consider radical options.

You should be wary of creating teams or business units that are too large. If you have more than, say, 10 fee earners in a team it can often be difficult to have effective team meetings and people can easily feel inhibited from speaking. The ideal size of a team will to a degree depend on the nature of the work; however, a partner or senior fee earner leading six to eight other fee earners is arguably a good size for many areas of work.

There will be exceptions, especially in bulk areas of work such as mortgage repossession; however, even large, highly automated, departments will normally be organised into smaller teams, perhaps of eight to 10 people.

Management structure and leadership

It is essential that firms have an effective management structure and an appropriate form of leadership. Indeed, leadership, and the development of an appropriate culture and ethos are some of the features that often mark out the more successful firms from others.

No doubt you will be aware of a number of styles of management from the history of your own firm or from others in your town or city. These may include:

- the benevolent dictator – the traditional senior partner typical of most firms in the past;
- the complete democracy that often follows the retirement of the once all-powerful senior partner;
- the committee-based system with representatives from the various parts of the firm, introduced when it became clear that democracy does not work;
- a more clearly defined structure with responsibility delegated to specific partners, perhaps with a managing partner, when it is realised that committee-based management is not much better than democracy!

The challenge is to find a style and structure that are appropriate to your firm and that suit its culture.

The overall aim and purpose of your firm's management structure should be to:

- help the partners realise their aspirations for the firm, in particular with regard to profitability, both in the short term and also in the longer term;
- enable the partners to concentrate on the important issues facing the firm rather than day-to-day matters;
- provide leadership and a sense of direction;
- use partner time effectively;
- get things done.

In essence its function is twofold:

- to ensure the smooth running of the firm;
- to enable the firm to move forward and develop.

Once there are more than, say, 10 people in a firm there is a need for someone to spend at least part of their time on the management of the firm. The form this will take will vary according to the personalities involved and the nature of the practice, but there is generally a need for someone to take a lead and to get things done.

In very small firms all the partners are likely to be involved in the firm's management, with each taking responsibility for certain areas. This can work well; however, as discussed previously, partners should be wary of getting unnecessarily involved in administration. You should also try to avoid simply allocating a task to everyone. Instead, try to play to each person's strengths and let each person concentrate on what they are good at. If one of your partners hates management, and is poor at it, why spend hours trying to change their personality?

As firms become larger, perhaps with 10 to 15 partners, they normally begin to develop a structure that is more 'corporate'. This may include a managing partner, but is as likely to be based on a small executive – normally of two or three partners who run the firm on a day-to-day basis, reporting back monthly to the full partner meetings. Such an executive typically would meet with key support staff – the practice manager or cashier – each week.

Finding the right management structure in firms with fewer than 15 partners can be difficult for the following reasons:

- the firm is probably too small to be able to afford professional managers;
- it is often difficult to justify too much partner time being spent on management;
- the need for better management is often not appreciated by all the partners;
- there can be a reluctance to bring in an external advisor to assist because of concerns about the likely cost.

However, a firm with, say, 10 to 15 partners, with a total staff ranging from 60 to 150, often in more than one office, is actually a complex business and one that needs a lot of management time to be successful.

Regardless of the size of firm, departments, teams and business units need to form part of the reporting structure. Each should have a team leader or department head reporting to the managing partner or the executive.

As indicated earlier, a good management structure should not simply achieve the smooth day-to-day running of the firm as it is now. It should aim to go beyond this and to help the firm to move forward. This requires leadership and a degree of drive.

Of course, many partners do not like the idea of being led or managed, as most managing partners will confirm! Leadership in law firms, indeed in most professional firms, is therefore different from that generally seen in commercial or industrial companies.

Often, when partners consider the issues of management and leadership, they begin by visualising military or political role models. However, the style of leadership characterised by people such as Winston Churchill or Margaret Thatcher is rarely successful within a law firm. It is seldom an effective way of motivating professional people – especially partners. Many partners, particularly in larger firms, can testify to the demotivating effect this, often arrogant, style of leadership can have. More appropriate styles, and the characteristics of a successful managing partner, are discussed in Chapter 2.

SUMMARY

1. Do not lose sight of the key factors for success: a sense of focus on the markets you serve; recruiting and retaining good people; client service; and generating sufficient profit.

2. Constantly remind your partners of the difference between management and administration – ensure their time is concentrated on the former.

3. Periodically, perhaps every three to five years, review your firm's operational structure: how you are organised into offices, departments and teams. Challenge the status quo – is it appropriate for the future?

4. Following this review, consider the type of management structure needed to manage this operational structure – and be radical in your thinking.

5. Define the roles and make sure the right people are running your firm.

6.   Get these people to lead the development of annual business and marketing plans and translate these into individual plans for each person.

7.   Monitor the plans and revise them – normally on a quarterly basis.

Notes

1   *Managing Partner*, July/August 2001.
2   Word document on disk: 'Questionnaire – Partner perceptions of their firm'.

2

The managing partner

The strength of leadership within a firm is normally one of the key factors that determines long-term success. The style of that leadership is fundamental to the happiness and cohesiveness of the partnership.

Most firms with more than, say, 10 to 15 partners decide that the most effective way of managing their firm is to appoint a managing partner. In firms with fewer than 20 partners this person will often work on management part-time, although there are exceptions to this. In firms with more than 20 partners it is generally a full-time position.

Once appointed, most managing partners realise that there is more to the job than being in charge of the administration, as sometimes envisaged by their fellow partners. They begin to understand that providing leadership and direction is just as important, although that may not be appreciated, or even wanted, by some of their partners.

The choice of who should be managing partner is not always obvious. In particular, firms are often unclear about what the job should cover, the personal skills needed if it is to be done successfully, and how much time will be required. In some firms the person who shouts the loudest gets the job, in others the highest billing partner, in yet others it is simply the most senior partner.

The job of managing partner can be a difficult and sometimes lonely one. This has been made worse in that most managing partners, at least in recent years, have had little training or preparation for the role, and have received relatively little support from their colleagues.

The difficult aspects of the job

The job has a number of frustrations, and many will identify with the comments of a group of managing partners – from firms ranging from eight to 40 equity partners – who were asked about the principal difficulties and frustrations they faced in undertaking their management role.[1] Their comments follow:

> One or two difficult people and problems can sometimes outweigh the positive; the economy is not predictable; clients can have unreasonable demands which encourages wheels to fall off.

Fee earners, including team leaders and senior partners who do not perform effectively the administrative and management tasks delegated to them. Lack of real sanctions!

The need sometimes to persuade 20+ people to do something. Partner interference/subversion of plans.

Succession; premises; conflict between management duties and client demands. Getting decisions at partnership level. Getting policies implemented firm-wide. Recruitment. Statutory and similar requirements – employment, money laundering, financial services, etc., etc.

Authority to enforce agreed decisions with other partners; partners making decisions without consideration of impact on whole firm; resistance of partners to change/innovation, and to accept that standards imposed on staff should also apply to themselves.

Balancing the time spent as managing partner and professional work; the unrealistic expectation of partners who want to be part of the management of the firm by being involved in day-to-day decisions; the same partners being dilatory in carrying out requests of the managing partner or following laid down procedure; not enough hours in the day.

Ensuring effective communication; dealing with insecurities on the part of partners.

Partners' unwillingness to accept/embrace change; resistance to management; danger of proceeding at pace of the slowest to come on board.

The nature of the partnership structure is unwieldy.

A dysfunctional management team; insufficient time to undertake it properly; a lack of appreciation of management issues on the part of other partners and staff; no qualifications or training in the necessary skills of herding cats.

In summary, the difficult areas were primarily concerned with:

- fellow partners:
  - who are underperforming,
  - who do not manage effectively or interfere,
  - lack of sanction over them,
  - getting agreement from them;
- getting people to change;
- lack of time.

Most of the respondents worked full-time (or virtually full-time) on management, but some still had sizeable caseloads. Some of the comments reflect the limitations of partnership itself as a vehicle, whilst others reflect the difficulty of managing a business which is evolving and in which the job of managing partner is itself changing. Several of the comments highlight the particular issues of levels of authority and lack of sanction over fellow partners.

Managing partner authority levels

The problems many managing partners experience stem from the partnership failing to agree the role and responsibilities of the job, and the levels of authority the managing partner has.

Whilst firms will vary in the authority delegated to individual partners, there will always be some decisions that are reserved for the whole partnership, or at least a majority, such as:

- the appointment of new partners;
- the removal of a partner;
- a merger with another firm;
- major decisions relating to property.

At the opposite extreme there will be a large number of minor decisions that the managing partner would be allowed to take alone, such as:

- the appointment of replacement support staff;
- agreements with routine trade suppliers;
- approval of overtime working;
- minor capital expenditure.

Between these two are a range of other decisions that a managing partner may be authorised to decide on their own such as:

- the appointment of additional staff;
- capital expenditure – up to a pre-agreed limit;
- staff salary increases;
- selection of bankers, accountants.

The key issue is to agree (in writing) what the managing partner can do, what they have to consult the board or executive about, and what they must take to a full partner meeting. It is a very good idea to insert figures into this document. Several of the managing partners had no limits specified; where there were such limits, the figures varied widely, as the following shows:

- £5,000;
- management board has authority to spend up to £20,000;

- £100,000;
- £150,000;
- no limit, but acting within the budget and not to appoint or dismiss partners;
- no formal limit – would consult on major expenditure.

Sanction over fellow partners

Many of the hardest problems a managing partner has to deal with concern fellow partners and are often aggravated by the lack of any real sanction over a fellow partner. This is a particular problem with a partner who is underperforming, or, worse, is being uncooperative.

Your partnership agreement will have provisions for expulsion of a partner, but these are unlikely to help in the event of one who is underperforming or uncooperative. Of course, these two very different situations are likely to require very different solutions.

Most professionals have phases in their careers where their performance is poor, and usually the problem passes and matters improve. Occasionally the problem is more serious and long term and can be the result of other underlying difficulties, such as:

- long-term changes in the market resulting in changed patterns and volumes of work – as has happened in recent years in personal injury, both claimant and defendant;
- the introduction of new technology or working methods to which partners may find it difficult to adjust;
- problems at home, especially marital;
- stress, depression or other forms of illness;[2]
- a perceived pressure from younger partners.

Invariably the starting point for dealing with underperformance is a willingness to talk with the partner and to listen to their concerns. The problem may take many months to resolve and may require many face-to-face sessions, but provided the person still has a positive attitude towards the firm the effort is generally worthwhile.

The more difficult areas, where the lack of sanction is most missed, is where partners are simply being unhelpful and uncooperative. The critical factor in dealing with this type of situation is often the strength of the managing partner's own authority within the firm and the level of support they have amongst the partnership as a whole.

The situation can be complicated if there are divisions between partners, but if the managing partner has the backing of the partners at least a start can be made in tackling the problem. Once again, the starting point is discussion with the person concerned with a view to listening to their perspective and trying to negotiate progress. Often, even the most unreasonable person has an element of justification in their cause.

The managing partner will need good people skills in this type of situation, and the approach taken will depend on the culture and size of the firm. The general rule, however, is not to duck the problem or avoid it, because it is unlikely to go away and can easily result in a terrible example to others that simply serves to undermine management within the firm.

Where direct discussion fails to bring results, an alternative tactic can be a general change in management or working methods, such as:

- appraisals and development reviews being extended to include partners in order to provide a forum for regular discussion about a partner's performance;
- greater openness about financial performance so as to provide 'gentle embarrassment' and a degree of peer pressure, especially if such information is made available to all members within the team;
- monthly marketing reports to be produced by all fee earners and circulated for information to all members of a team, once again to create peer pressure.

Perhaps the final weapon in a managing partner's armoury is profit allocation, which sometimes appears to be the only thing that makes an impact. The problem is that unless you have already agreed a basis of allocation that includes an element according to performance, it is difficult to introduce when at least one partner will vote against it. Ensure, therefore, that you have negotiated an element of allocation according to performance and have agreed how this is to be measured long before a problem arises.

The good parts of the job

Having dwelt on some of the problem areas, I should add that being managing partner also has its good points! The same group of managing partners were also asked about the things they enjoyed about their management role:

Decision making; the job fits my abilities far better than being a lawyer; demonstrating tangible benefits to my partners gained by them from my role; not being subject to constant client demands and therefore being able to dictate my priorities; finding ways to create satisfaction at all levels (but not always managing to do so!).

Sheer variety of issues to deal with. Satisfaction of controlling various strands of activity. Multi-faceted role.

Making things work; stimulation of employees; freedom to get on with it; having a chance to make a difference.

Success of firm; team working; strategic planning; seeing and assisting the development of people within the firm; business development; client care.

Driving business forward and achieving success for firm – new building, merger, profitability, recruiting and keeping excellent staff, developing new business areas. Giving something back to the community in a way that reflects our business ethos. Working with people.

Having seen the firm develop over the last seven years; notwithstanding frustration with individual partners, being part of a balanced partnership; ensuring the firm is run in accordance with, and achieving its budget each year; witnessing the younger members of the firm successfully develop their careers; working with an excellent management team; the people I work with!

The people in the firm.

Energy, support and enthusiasm of non-partner staff; seeing people develop and take on responsibility; at most optimistic – seeing changes happen and 'management' making a positive difference.

The ability to influence and shape the direction of the firm.

An ability to shape the future of the firm; variety; an input into the development of staff.

These comments confirm that the job can be fun and enjoyable – provided the ground rules have been agreed, and everyone understands what the job entails. They also illustrate that some managing partners quite quickly begin to enjoy the job more than being a lawyer, and the issue of retirement as managing partner, and what to do afterwards, can become problematic. Particular themes in these comments include:

- the variety the job offers;
- the satisfaction to be gained from developing others;
- the opportunity to influence the shape and direction of the firm;
- the satisfaction of seeing the business develop.

The qualities of a successful managing partner

It is important that the right person is made managing partner, and the starting point is therefore to define the job and the type of person required. The group of managing partners quoted previously were also asked what they considered the principal qualities of a managing partner to be. Their responses included:

> The ability to make decisions and carry them through; good communication skills and creation of team spirit; reasonable understanding of finances; leadership; ability to use a broad brush; very good problem-solving skills; lateral thinking both as to strategy and in all other areas; ear to the ground.

> Organisational flair; business acumen; incisive thinking; ability to make decisions (and stand by them); clear vision of firm's strategy; ability to lead and command respect; to be sympathetic and approachable; to be articulate and numerate.

> Patience; more patience; vision; decisiveness; communication skills.

> Resilience – to bounce back and carry on; tenacity – in the face of resistance; humour – by the bucketload; confidence – in the face of relentless questioning; absolute clarity of thought – to back up decisions; outstanding communication skills – to explain them; excellent back-up – in support team; organisation and planning skills – for implementation.

> Vision; patience; energy; tact; determination; financial awareness; good communication skills; pragmatism.

> Interpersonal skills; integrity and consistency; drive, enthusiasm, energy, passion; clarity of purpose and ability to gain agreement; shared understanding of goals; ambition for firm; selflessness and ability to push forward others; compassion and firmness/resolve.

> To be professional and of the highest integrity; to have a good management team and to delegate effectively; to be organised and proactive rather than reactive; to be prepared to listen to others and where appropriate to support their view notwithstanding it may not be your preferred view; to be prepared to take hard decisions; pastoral care for staff and partners alike; to be aware of opportunities to develop the firm; to run a profitable firm within the ethos and culture adopted by the partnership. PS: I do not pretend to achieve all of these!

> Honesty/sincerity; able communicator; even-handedness; arrogance that your ideas are as good as anyone's; humility – a willingness to admit when things are wrong or not working.

> The respect of his partners; the ability to motivate his staff; the ability to implement decisions; understanding of the business and its market; ability to put together and work with a good management team.

> Vision; an ability and wish to listen; stamina; thick hide; people skills; confidence – and self-belief; authority/ability to lead; to enjoy it!

Some of the key factors are therefore:

- to be a good communicator;
- to be able to get things done;
- a sense of vision;
- to be good at making decisions;
- to be able to lead;
- patience;
- determination;
- energy – and a sense of humour!

Michael Shaw, managing partner of Cobbetts, a leading Manchester firm, identifies 10 key qualities a managing partner should have:[3]

- **Arrogance** – you simply have to believe that at least your ideas for the future of the firm are as good as, or better than, those of anybody else. Of course, if you are like me then you will probably suffer from permanent self-doubt (that you can't share) and arrogance should not stop you from listening to (and using) everyone else's ideas;
- **Credibility** – consultants and academics often seem to suggest that it is bizarre that the usual qualification for leadership is the individual's history for achieving very high billings. Of course high billings in themselves don't make a leader but it does provide a basis for credibility. There has been a clear record of commitment and achievement for the firm and the last thing you can ever stand to risk is someone within the firm saying, '. . . but you don't know what it's like at the coal face';
- **Honesty** – unless you possess other superhuman abilities, dishonesty and insincerity are spotted instantly by those within the firm and your clients. This is applicable on an individual basis and also collectively as a firm. We all get things wrong and certainly I have found it actually does some good when you are prepared to tell everybody else that is the case;
- **Respect** – this is not so much respect for you, but the respect you have for everybody else. If that is instilled within the firm, then the recognition of potential on the part of everyone regardless of status is axiomatic. Neither you, your partners, nor your qualified staff has a monopoly on wisdom. Some of our youngest support staff have the most profound understanding of clients' needs and how they should be fulfilled. If you do not recognise the potential of all, you will not bring out the best;
- **Courage (or recklessness – I'm not sure which)** – our training teaches us to abandon creativity and avoid risk taking, but in trying to create a lead you can't follow the herd. Yes, you can learn lessons from others but what is right for your firm is quite different to any other. Accept that some things will work, but not everything;
- **Security** – insecurity has to be abandoned both in your role as leader and also in the roles of others within the firm. Undoubtedly, personal insecurity tends to be the biggest barrier to change and I have found the biggest demand upon my time is talking to colleagues to help them face those hurdles and build their confidence;

- **Open-mindedness** – be prepared to listen to new ideas from whatever source and don't interpret a difference of opinion as being criticism;
- **Communication, communication, communication . . . ad infinitum** – recognise that your firm is populated by bright people who will generally cooperate fully – once they have gained an understanding of what you are trying to do;
- **Friendships** – you need your friends to tell you when you've got it wrong, and your best friends to tell you when it's OK, because nobody else will;
- **Modesty** – yes, take credit while it's going, but don't let the necessary display of self-belief delude you. Above all else, remember that the moment you feel smug, you have failed.

This set of skills will be found in a limited number of candidates; however, they provide an indication of the type of person you should be looking for. Successful managing partners are normally equity partners – it is very difficult for a salaried partner to have the necessary authority – and they should if possible be part of the power base of the firm.

Do not assume your managing partner is going to be one of the most senior partners in the firm. Be prepared to look further down the partner list, perhaps to someone in his or her late thirties. In particular, consider your women partners – most managing partners are male, yet women often have much better people skills than their male colleagues – they can be more sensitive to feelings and better at picking up non-verbal communication.

Also, have in mind the issue of succession and look for a wide range of personal skills in your future partners. Be prepared to embrace ideas such as personality profiling to get a better assessment of prospective partners and senior staff.

Above all, be clear about the role, the level of authority, the term of office, and what the person is expected to do after ceasing to be managing partner.

The role of the managing partner

Many firms do not specify how long the term of a managing partner should be, and how many terms they may serve, but they should. Two years is normally too short, five years is probably too long. The optimal term is normally three years, and a managing partner should serve two – at the most three – terms. It is often said that a managing partner only really starts to get the hang of the job towards the end of the first term, and then goes on to do a good job in the second. At a very early stage the managing partner should begin thinking who their successor may be and should spend several years training this person to take on the role. There may be more than one candidate, which is a good position to be in, and these people should be given every opportunity to develop and hone their management skills.

Unless your managing partner is an exceptional being, after six or nine years a new person is normally needed to provide fresh energy and drive. This can of course be difficult because, as indicated previously, some managing partners begin to enjoy the role much more than that of being a lawyer. Also, some firms are, in effect, controlled by one or two partners who may control over 50 per cent of the voting rights. It can seem impossible for these people not to be in charge but there comes a time when fresh ideas are needed and a way has to be found to bring new people in.

In firms with more than 15 to 20 partners, the role of managing partner is almost always full-time, although many still do some fee earning in order to keep in touch with the law and their clients. In firms with fewer than 15 partners, some managing partners also spend most of their time managing, but many will also undertake a significant amount of fee earning – at least 50 per cent. In firms with fewer than eight partners it is rare to find full-time managing partners. Those involved in management invariably spend most of their time fee earning – and finish up working very long days.

Managing partners can sometimes combine high fee earning with a relatively small amount of time spent on management by being very well organised and being able to clearly separate the two roles. One managing partner simply devoted every Friday to management, but was able to do so because she spent the day at a different office, had very good managers responsible for finance and personnel, and an excellent personal assistant.

Full-time managing partners (and other partners) frequently work 10- to 12-hour days. Where they have a significant fee-earning role their hours tend to be longer because of the need to combine the two roles. One managing partner of a four-office, 30-fee-earner firm commented that she did her client work during the day and started her management work at 5 p.m.

The job typically involves:

- taking responsibility for the firm's administration and management. All the firm's professional managers (finance, personnel, marketing, IT, etc.) normally report to the managing partner;
- taking responsibility for the firm's financial performance including overall profitability, and also borrowings, in particular the bank overdraft or balance;
- taking overall responsibility for achieving the objectives set out in the firm's business plan.

Normally the heads of each department or team will report to the managing partner, and may form a small 'board' with him or her.

When defining the role you should also consider:

- the level of fees (if any) that the managing partner is expected to bill;
- the managing partner's authority limit – how much they are allowed to spend without approval of the partnership. As discussed earlier, many firms have no formal level, but the managing partner knows how much in practice they can spend. In a firm with around 15 partners this could be set at £20,000; in larger firms it could be £100,000. It depends entirely on the firm and its structure.

Life after managing partner

The issue of succession is sometimes difficult as a managing partner reaches the end of their second, or perhaps, third term. Theoretically, the concept has been to do the job for six or nine years and then return full-time to fee earning, perhaps at the same time taking on the role of senior partner. Unfortunately, it is not always that easy. Two main problems can arise.

The first flows from the greater need, especially in larger firms, for the job to be full-time, and that has resulted in many managing partners losing their previously close relationships with their client bases and becoming out of touch with the law. It can then be difficult to rebuild a client base, in particular when you may previously have been one of your firm's highest fee earners, and especially in firms that focus too much on personal fee levels. The second problem arises from the fact that some good managing partners find they like management more than fee earning, and are probably better at it.

It is fairly important then for managing partners to review at intervals during their term of office their longer-term career plans and to ensure they are able to return to fee earning if they wish. Although a managing partner may be full-time, in practice it is always better to carry a small workload – perhaps 20 per cent – and retain a small number of clients. Perhaps the most useful person a managing partner can have (in addition to an excellent secretary) is a good assistant, a reliable solicitor who works with them dealing with the detail of their client work whilst they manage the firm.

The managing partner's relationship with their clients will change and will be less hands-on, but there may be one or two clients with whom they are still involved in the detail so as to keep up to date with the law.

It is especially useful to acquire the occasional new client to avoid the problem of a lack of confidence in winning new clients on returning to fee earning. In reality, if you have been able to use your time as managing partner effectively, you will have become a far better marketer and will have been moving in a much greater circle of contacts than previously, and should be able to use this to your advantage.

With careful planning, therefore, it should be possible to return to fee earning, albeit in a different role and at a different level. The importance of maximising the potential of an ex-managing partner should not be understated – you will have made contacts that are invaluable to you and to the firm as a whole, and will now have time to exploit them.

CASE STUDY   **Managing partner**

I took on the role of managing partner at the age of 51, which is perhaps older than many who take on the role. Like most managing partners I had a fee-earning role which settled down after a year to a 50/50 split. I have greatly enjoyed my period in office having seen the firm develop to twice its size seven years ago and with an exciting future, I believe, ahead of it.

It has, of course, had its ups and downs and I suppose the most interesting and at times frustrating moments have been in how to handle one's own partners. That has certainly presented a challenge.

As I plan to hand over the reins I do so with a mixture of emotions. As a firm we have been good at planning the future so I have known two years in advance of the handover.

I consider one of the most important features to be the relationship between the managing partner and senior partner. I consider that, by and large, I have enjoyed a good relationship with the present senior partner, and my successor as managing partner is not only someone who is a good friend but is someone in whom I have the greatest confidence in handing over the mantle and with whom I shall also maintain an excellent relationship.

I have been working on the handover for the last year thus enabling the new managing partner to shadow me, which I believe is essential for good management. When he takes over on 1 June I shall obviously miss the cut and thrust of the job but equally realise that I must let go but be around if my successor needs help and support as he takes over the role.

In some ways because I am taking over as senior partner until my retirement I shall still continue to have a 50/50 fee-earning and senior partner role and thus my fee earning in that sense is unlikely to be felt whereas I suspect many of my contemporaries will find life more difficult as they concentrate purely on fee-earning. I think that at the age of 58-plus I would find it pretty challenging to go back to full fee earning having enjoyed as I have done my role as managing partner!

In some firms there can be a real issue in who is going to take over. There may be a genuine lack of candidates. If this is an issue it is something a managing partner needs to work on early in their second term – to begin nurturing and bringing on much younger people and developing the skills of the people they have. There will be other firms, especially smaller ones, where the firm has one key equity partner who effectively 'owns' the firm.

Even in the latter case, a point is invariably reached where fresh blood and ideas are needed. We all become stale with time if we continue doing exactly the same job.

The skill is subtly to move on, to continue to manage but in a different way, and to harness the energy and enthusiasm of your younger partners. It is sometimes especially important to listen to your colleagues and pick up the signals that change is needed. Move at your own timing and with dignity rather than being shoved!

SUMMARY

1. Spend some time defining the role of managing partner and ensure all the partners agree to it.
2. Be clear what the authority levels of the managing partner are.
3. Try to ensure you select the best person for the job – not the person who shouts loudest or who is the highest fee earner in the firm.
4. Provide your managing partner with support and try not to undermine their position and decisions.
5. At an early stage in the managing partner's second term (even their first) they should begin to identify possible successors and start training them. They need to try to create opportunities for their successor to gain experience and to make mistakes they can learn from.

Notes

1   Management Forum 2001 held at Le Manoir aux Quat' Saisons, Oxfordshire. Responses to pre-forum questionnaires.
2   If you are concerned that one of your partners (or indeed any of your solicitors) is suffering from stress or depression, alcohol/drug abuse, has an eating disorder or any other health problem, you can contact LawCare for confidential advice on 0800 279 6888 or e-mail them at admin@lawcare.org.uk
3   Originally published in *Managing Partner*, July/August 2001.

The senior partner and other partners' roles in management

As well as having a managing partner, good firms require a management structure that provides functional responsibility for areas such as finance, marketing, human resources and IT; and also provides line management through to the fee earners.

Finance, marketing and staff partners

The areas that need to be managed in order for a firm to function on a day-to-day basis are normally grouped under the following headings:

- finance
- marketing
- human resources
- IT.

There might also be other headings such as library, premises and insurances, but the four listed above are the principal areas for most firms.

Eventually, as firms grow, professionals may be appointed to lead and manage each of these areas. In very small firms the managing or senior partner may deal with all of these areas personally, perhaps assisted by various members of staff. Between these extremes individual partners normally head up each area, reporting back to the partners' meeting or to a small executive.

Once again it is important to spell out the responsibilities of each role and to agree their authority.

Normally, at the start of each year, a budget should be agreed for each area, and responsibility for spending that budget should be vested in the appropriate partner. In practice he or she would consult and discuss ideas with others but essentially that person should be in charge of the budget, and would only need to come back to the partners if it needed to be increased – or perhaps to explain major underspends.

The actual roles would comprise the following.

Finance partner

The finance partner has a key role to play in the management of a firm, often the most important after the managing partner. Many smaller firms will combine the role of managing partner and finance partner.

The finance partner is essentially the equivalent of a finance director in a company – the person who monitors and controls the financial performance of the firm and its profitability. It is a potentially difficult role as it will, on occasion, require that pressure be put on fellow partners or departments to improve their performance. In some firms it can be difficult, at least in the initial stages, for a partner to fulfil the role without outside help, perhaps from the firm's accountants, a management consultant or a non-executive advisor such as a retired bank manager.

The role of the finance partner is likely to include:

- setting an achievable yet challenging budget;
- monitoring the firm's financial performance against budget both at departmental and office level, and for the firm as a whole, and reporting on the financial position to the partner meetings;
- overseeing the cashier's or accounts department, ensuring that the management accounts are produced speedily, that they highlight the key figures that need to be monitored, and helping the partners to understand these figures;
- monitoring debtors, unbilled disbursements and cash levels.

Human resources – or staff partner

The staff partner will be responsible for trying to ensure that:

- the firm makes full use of each person's strengths and that each person contributes fully to achieving the firm's goals;
- partner and staff roles are clearly defined;
- systems are in place and working for recruitment, appraisals, training and development and succession;
- communications within the firm are effective.

It is important that firms maintain good records regarding their staff, and an important initial task for a staff partner is to make sure these are working properly. Some of these, such as training records, can be maintained by each member of staff and are simply updated by them every time they attend a course.

Marketing partner

The marketing partner should:

- ensure marketing plans are developed for each department and office, and for the firm as a whole;
- monitor and coordinate progress.

The role is primarily concerned with coordination and motivation and making sure that sufficient time is allocated to marketing by the other partners and fee earners. The idea is not to appoint your most gregarious partner and let him or her attend endless dinners with accountants and bankers – and assume you have dealt with marketing, neither is it to do all the firm's marketing yourself. Ensure, rather, that others are doing it.

Part of the plan will be to consider what form of marketing is appropriate for each area of work – and it will differ. For the insolvency and corporate lawyers at the leading law firms in cities such as Leeds and Manchester, much of their marketing is undertaken in a small number of city centre pubs adjacent to the offices of the main accountants. Links are established at all levels, between partners, assistants, trainees and support staff.

For claimant insurance lawyers, their work may flow from newspaper or radio advertising, or from 'claims farms'. For conveyancers, it may be dependent on strong links with particular estate agents, or through your firm's own estate agency.

Marketing partners are frequently selected because they are natural marketers and tend not to find the role onerous. They see it as an extension of something they do anyway and they view marketing as something all fee earners should do more of. Sometimes, however, although they enjoy it personally, and are good at marketing their own particular areas of work, they can find it difficult to relate to other areas and fail to appreciate fully the need to adapt the style of marketing to the different areas of work.

It can be useful for each department or team to identify someone to coordinate marketing within the team, and these people can then meet, perhaps monthly, as a marketing committee or working party, to coordinate marketing across the firm. This meeting would be chaired by the marketing partner, the committee would have its own budget, and may well have a marketing assistant to undertake much of the detailed marketing administration.

IT partner

The first task for the IT partner will be to draw up an IT strategy for the firm that:

- is based upon the firm's business plan;

- sets out what is required over, say, the next three years based upon an assessment of each person's needs and consideration of how better use of IT could improve their performance and profitability;
- prioritises the firm's needs according to what can actually be afforded.

Subsequently the role will include:

- making sure everyone receives appropriate training – not just when the system is delivered, but on an ongoing basis to ensure the system is being used to the full;
- ensuring effective support and maintenance is provided;
- keeping abreast of new developments and ensuring that the system is updated as appropriate to take advantage of them.

IT partners often select themselves because they are very interested in IT and count it among their outside interests. This is not necessarily a good qualification because such people often get too immersed in the detail. It can sometimes be very useful to have someone in-house who can deal with day-to-day IT problems, although many firms find it is better to out-source most of their IT support.

Team leaders and heads of department

In addition to the functional areas of responsibility discussed above, the firm's management structure should ensure there is clear line responsibility from the managing partner through to the individual fee earners. This is normally achieved through team leaders or heads of department.

In most firms these are important positions because these are the people who do much of the leadership and management within a firm. A good managing partner will often delegate much of their responsibility to these managers, and their job, at least in part, becomes one of encouraging and leading the team leaders.

In some firms, traditionally the job of head of department revolved around administrative tasks such as making sure timesheets were completed on time. The task envisaged here is different – it is concerned with leading and developing their part of the business: in effect, managing partner of their team or department. It is an excellent training ground for future managing partners.

The senior partner

The role of senior partner is an important, sometimes neglected position in a firm of solicitors. Nowadays, too, they are not always that 'senior' – they are getting younger, and the concept of the job is changing.

In the 1980s, most firms did not have a managing partner, and were instead managed and run, often very successfully, by their senior partner who took on a much more hands-on and executive role than is seen today.

The management problems of a number of firms today have their roots in the retirement of these all-powerful figures who were sometimes very autocratic and often poor at developing and training their successors. In some instances the most likely successors would leave the firm because very autocratic senior partners could be difficult to work with. They clashed with the strong personalities below them or simply stifled the development of the immediate level of partners below. This has left an age gap in the partnership – the natural successors to the senior partner are missing and are instead running other firms nearby!

Another result is that partners who were happy to leave everything to the senior partner – sometimes to the detriment of his, or occasionally her, health – failed to learn and pick up the management skills and acumen they needed. Along the way they picked up an impression that management was more complicated than it actually is, and this sometimes fuels a feeling of inadequacy today.

Nowadays many senior partners still play an important part in the development of their firms; however, much of the day-to-day management has been passed to the managing partner, and also much of the strategic management. The first task, therefore, is to define the role.

At one extreme, the job of senior partner, or chairman, as it is often known, comprises just:

- dealing with complaints;
- external projection of the firm ('awarding the firm's prize at speech days of the local school');
- chairing partner meetings.

Others use the role in a more proactive way to complement and support the managing partner:

- as someone whose job it is to think about the longer-term development of the firm ('a brief to look at the longer term and chair our strategy committee');
- as advocate of partner relations (a 'partners' partner');
- as a sounding board.

Obviously the needs of firms will vary; however, this latter type of role is a very effective way of strengthening a firm's overall management and utilising the experience of more senior partners.

Traditionally, the senior partner was the first name on the firm's letterhead, but this is changing:

> Something used to happen to my previously very reasonable colleagues once they became senior partner. Their character seemed to change and people who had been perfectly pleasant became impossible to work with.

In many cases today the position of senior partner is an elected one – for perhaps two five-year terms – and the people who fill the position are frequently retired managing partners. It is a tremendous way of capitalising on the skills and experience they learnt whilst being managing partner. The average age is also coming down, from over 60 to mid-fifties or younger.

The managing partner/senior partner relationship

The relationship between senior and managing partner can be difficult to manage, but has the potential to be one of the most important factors in the success of a managing partner's term of office.

As discussed earlier, the job of managing partner is sometimes very lonely and the senior partner can be an invaluable sounding board, especially with regard to problems with fellow partners. The senior partner may well have been there before and will thus have experience that can be drawn on. The case studies below illustrate the senior partner's roles.

CASE STUDY   **Senior partner (I)**

The senior partner has two key roles in our firm.

The first is the relationship within the management team where the senior partner must fulfil the role of a non-executive chairman and only get dragged into management issues when there is serious dissent or strong leadership is required to push through difficult decisions. The senior partner must not be regarded as the managing partner's echo and always there to support him against the world. The managing partner must earn the senior partner's support and accept that there are times when they will be at odds. Only in this way can the senior partner properly be seen as the 'partners' partner' throughout the firm.

Secondly, the external appearance of the relationship is important, both for the firm itself and for the outside world. The firm itself must understand that the managing partner is the CEO of the firm, whilst the senior partner is the father figure and ambassador who is wheeled out for all the usual state occasions and is the recognisable embodiment of the firm. So far as external relationships are concerned, the managing partner's role will be largely unseen as clients are not concerned about how the firm manages itself, as long as it does it properly. The senior partner will be more visible through his ambassadorial role.

The senior partner can also very usefully play the role of 'partners' partner' – someone the partners can turn to when they are not happy with how things are going. He or she can often diffuse a problem at an early stage and avoid a direct conflict with the managing partner.

| CASE STUDY | **Senior partner (II)** |

I believe that the senior partner has an important role in a professional partnership not least because his position is quite different from that of the managing partner.

Whereas the managing partner must inevitably become immersed in the day-to-day affairs of the firm, the senior partner can (and should) detach himself and therefore has the ability to provide the overview. A good example of this is the role the senior partner can fulfil as chairman of partners' meetings and the management board. In these situations the managing partner will be seeking approval for a range of actions which relate to the driving forward and development of the business. Frequently he will be challenged and always he can be held to account. The senior partner (whilst clearly not working against the direction chosen by the managing partner) must allow issues to be properly debated and try to ensure a satisfactory outcome.

The senior partner should have the 'ear' of partners and staff. He should act as mentor and confidante and be regarded as the court of final appeal in relation to personnel issues. This contrasts with the position of the managing partner who will not be able to be at arm's length to such an extent.

The senior partner also has an important role to play both amongst the firm's clients and within the wider community. He has (or must create) the time to put himself about and to be seen as the face of the firm in public. The managing partner is likely to be too embroiled in the running of the firm to allow him to do this. More importantly, however, the senior partner, almost invariably, will have been around longer and will therefore be better suited to an ambassadorial role.

In some cases the relationship can be difficult, especially if the senior partner had previously been managing partner and had wanted to continue in that role. It is only human to feel annoyance and irritation when a successor comes along with different ideas, but it is important, if the firm is to develop, not to frustrate things. It is especially important not to divide a partnership and work against a managing partner, although this can be difficult when points of principle are involved. The job of senior partner often calls for good interpersonal skills and a high degree of tact!

A senior partner/chairman is likely to chair some, but not necessarily all, partner meetings, and a working relationship has to be developed that does not sideline the managing partner at such times. A senior partner should ensure all partners have a chance to express their views, and sometimes needs to elicit them. It is remarkable how many partners do not speak at partner meetings, yet these people will have views, and the silent ones who nod and agree at the meeting and then do nothing afterwards can be a real problem. A good senior partner can help to bring these people out.

SUMMARY

1. Put in place a structure below the managing partner that covers the functional areas of finance, marketing, human resources and IT.
2. Put in place a structure of clear line management from the managing partner to fee earners via team leaders or heads of department.
3. Try to utilise the experience of your more senior partners and put in place a structure that enables them to work with and support the managing partner – to the overall benefit of the firm.

4

Professional managers and chief executives

A managing partner's success (and personal job satisfaction) is very much dependent on having high quality professional managers working with them and supporting them in their role.

The benefits of non-lawyer managers

As firms evolve and grow in size partners invariably spend an ever greater proportion of their time on management, some completely giving up the law. As they develop they move from employing a cashier, to recruiting a practice manager, and then professional managers – initially in finance, perhaps followed by personnel, marketing and IT. Many firms reach the point where at least some of the partners begin to question the cost of tying up so much partner time in management and ask whether the firm would not be better served by bringing in a chief executive.

High quality professional managers are central to the release of partner time from day-to-day management, and also to improving the quality of that management. There is an important distinction, however, between:

- a cashier;
- a practice manager;
- finance, personnel, marketing and IT professionals; and
- chief executives.

The first three can work very well; the latter is, so far at least, proving difficult to get right.

The appointment of a professional manager should be undertaken in the light of an overall review of the firm's management structure and should have the following aims:

- to improve the quality of the firm's management and administration;
- to free partner time from unnecessary involvement in administration.

When considering such an appointment, do not underestimate the potential benefits a good person can deliver, and do not try to economise on the salary package offered. There are relatively few good people around, so don't risk losing a good person by paying too little.

Cashiers

Most firms have a cashier and they are key to the smooth running of the practice.

The exception is some small firms in London, where it is quite common to subcontract cashiers to do the bookkeeping. The bookkeeper might come into the firm for perhaps one or two days a week, depending on the volume of work. This is a good way of enabling small firms to afford a bookkeeper, and is especially appropriate for legal aid firms, who deal in relatively little client money.

At least one IT company recently has set up a remote bookkeeping service, and this can also work very well, especially for very small firms. For one sole practitioner, for example, the cost of such a service was very much less than employing his own cashier, and holiday cover ceased to be a problem.

A good cashier who understands the accounts rules requirements is essential for any firm. You need to have confidence that this is under control. It is important your cashier is qualified and receives good technical support and he or she should be encouraged to join a professional body such as the Institute of Legal Cashiers (ILCA).[1]

In small firms the cashier will spend most of their time posting transactions during the month, running the payroll, dealing with suppliers, producing month-end printouts, chasing overdue debtors, dealing with computer problems, VAT, PAYE, and so on. It is a time-consuming and often frustrating job, as the case study below shows.

CASE STUDY   **The cashier**

Having just one partner in your firm who is really interested and understanding about why we have to go into such detail when recording financial transactions can make a huge difference to the efficiency of an accounts department.

Basic things such as cheque requests arriving without matter numbers and/or the correct authorities, or cheques for banking submitted without identification, cause unnecessary telephone calls and interruptions to fee earners. I am never surprised to hear cashiers described as 'ogres' or 'dragons' by staff in other departments. It seems as if all we do is harass people. This is unfortunate but what else are we to do in order to comply with the accounts rules?

A sympathetic partner can be a bridge between the staff and the accounts department by stressing the importance of adhering to agreed systems and procedures.

The cashier's relationship with the reporting accountant is also important because we often have to liaise with them. It can be quite daunting having to ask for guidance but knowing that your request will be met with interest and a willingness to help is confidence boosting.

A computerised accounts system that is right for the practice is another huge bonus. Having the opportunity to be involved in its selection is invaluable and helps develop a good rapport with the supplier's trainers and helpline staff.

It is also good to know the ILCA is there behind us – we can ask them almost anything and be sure of getting the definitive answer.

The principal qualities of a good cashier are a detailed knowledge of the accounts rules, accurate and reliable accounting skills, familiarity and confidence with IT and, most important, honesty.

There is often a tendency to give the cashier more and more tasks to do, and some begin to struggle. You need to know and understand the person and know their limitations. Others are capable of much more, and these people can be developed to play a wider role in the firm's management. Frequently the cashier knows what should be done to improve profitability; however, they are sometimes not listened to or are considered too junior to be taken seriously. The cashier will normally report to the managing or finance partner, and it is the latter's job to listen to their ideas and use them to the full.

Practice managers

The drawback in very small firms is that the cashier invariably just does the bookkeeping, and much of the administration of the firm is still done by partners. The solution can be to employ a practice manager.

Many firms are starting to appoint such a person, often in addition to the cashier, to undertake a much wider management role, including staff issues, IT and virtually anything else the partners ask them to get involved in. Sometimes the cashier develops into this role, at other times it is undertaken by someone without any accountancy training.

Once again the problem can be that everything is dumped on this person and they soon sink under an impossible range of duties. The following job description is rather extreme but not uncommon:

> We are a well regarded firm that has grown rapidly over the last five years, and wish to appoint a practice manager who will be responsible to the managing partner for:
>
> - The supervision of an accounts department comprising two cashiers, and overall responsibility for compliance with all aspects of the Solicitors' Accounts Rules and the Law Society's Money Laundering regulations.
> - The maintenance of our contracts with the Legal Services Commission and compliance with LAFQAS/SQM and Lexcel.
> - Personnel and staff management.
> - Providing timely and meaningful management information for the managing partner to present at the partners' meeting.
> - Overseeing the firm's computer systems, website and intranet.
> - Helping the partners prepare the annual business plan.
> - Dealing with ad hoc projects on behalf of the partners.
>
> The successful candidate will be a key member of the management team.

Many practice managers were able to relate to the reaction of a particular practice manager of a 10-partner firm quoted in *Profitability and Financial Management*. When asked 'what's it like being a practice manager?', the reply was:

> An interesting question to which there is no easy answer. Interesting – sometimes; intellectually stimulating – rarely; a nightmare – most of the time! In what other field of endeavour can you work for employers who:
>
> - leave everything to the last minute or, preferably, until a week or two after the last minute;
> - think that their clients are irritants and that it is perfectly in order to keep them waiting for appointments and responses to letters, but will complain bitterly if they consider that they have been on the receiving end of poor customer care themselves;
> - treat their secretarial staff as though they are 'in service' and should be thankful to be treated as machines for little by way of reward;
> - take no interest in staff issues until it is their own secretary who has had enough and is leaving;
> - consider it is quite in order to totally disregard decisions taken at partner meetings, even those decisions they proposed/argued for/voted on themselves;
> - will happily write off thousands of pounds owed to the practice, usually because it was never chased up when it should have been, but will moan and groan at the need to spend a few pounds on an essential item of equipment;

- proudly boast to the outside world about their 'quality' service, but resist every attempt to adopt even basic quality controls;
- work incredibly hard themselves (because nobody can do the job as well as they can), often to the detriment of their health, yet lack the courage to remove partners who contribute little to the success and profitability of the practice;
- vote in one partner as managing partner who is prepared to attempt to sort out the mess and shoulder all the responsibilities, but then give him no support whatsoever.

So why continue working as a practice manager? It is a challenge and despite their many faults solicitors are generally pleasant people who, deep down, do want to get things 'sorted out' – I think!

Since 1998 when *Profitability and Financial Management* was published, most firms appear to have improved their use of practice managers, as illustrated in the following case study:

CASE STUDY   **Practice manager**

I have been in post in my role as a practice manager for nine months. Being a solicitor myself the working environment was familiar and so I didn't have to adjust in that sense.

What is clear, from my experience, and talking to other practice managers, or partnership secretaries (many of whom provide the same role), is that it's a job that requires flexibility. The role is still quite a new one for many small/medium-sized firms and is not always clearly defined, therefore the view of your role, and how far it does/doesn't extend or should/shouldn't extend means different things to different people within the firm.

The role is varied and there is no opportunity for boredom, as I have input into the functional areas of management, strategy, finance, human resources, and also operations (since I have been a fee earner myself). It's definitely challenging at times but that's positive in terms of my own personal development.

I feel as a practice manager my contribution and inputs are valued and it's a rewarding role for someone who likes dealing with people; after all let's not forget that's what management is all about!

The starting point for appointing a practice manager, and for getting it right from the outset, is, therefore, to be clear about the role and to prepare a realistic job description.

In a typical single-office high street firm with, say, 10 partners and a total of 60 or 70 people, the administration of the firm may come under two people, the accountant and the practice manager, both of whom report to the managing partner.

The staff in cashiers would report to the accountant, who would be responsible for:

- monthly and quarterly accounts;
- VAT, PAYE, etc.;
- dealing with suppliers;
- posting accounting transactions;
- petty cash;
- salaries;
- IT back-up;
- closing old files, and the billing of certain areas of work.

The receptionists, office juniors and cleaners would report to the practice manager. Secretaries would report to their head of department, but the practice manager would deal with all staff problems relating to secretarial and support staff. He or she would be responsible for:

- staff records and personnel;
- temporary staff;
- holidays;
- stationery;
- recruitment of secretaries and support staff;
- authorisation of any overtime by support staff;
- IT maintenance and technical problems;
- marketing support.

In this type of arrangement both the accountant and practice manager would meet with the managing partner at least weekly and would often form part of the management team running the firm on a day-to-day basis.

In order to get maximum benefit from the appointment of a practice manager:

- spend quite a bit of time getting the job description right. Don't give the person an impossible set of tasks to do because they will fail;
- be clear what the actual scope of the job is. Are you looking for a kind of 'super-cashier' who will actually spend most of their time on day-to day cashiering or do you want someone who will perform more of a management role;

- be clear who the person is going to report to. It is not possible to report to all 10 partners, even though you may run your firm as an equal partnership. Specify the person the practice manager is going to report to and agree their authority limits.

Professional managers

As firms get larger they invariably move beyond the stage where one person can fulfil the practice manager role, and professionals in each of the main areas are appointed.

Typically the first appointment is an accountant, partnership secretary or director of finance, followed often by personnel, marketing and IT professionals.

At this size of firm fewer mistakes tend to be made concerning the job specification; however, issues can arise around reporting structures, and whether there is still a need to have a staff or marketing partner.

The case studies that follow are all from firms with around 20 partners.

CASE STUDY   **Personnel manager (I)**

The partners of the firm, whilst very fair, today work under such time constraints and pressure that they are more than happy to have managers around them that can ease the burden of the day-to-day running of the practice, allowing them to carry out their legal work.

My job, looking after some 120 personnel is full of challenges – different from day to day. One must have the ability to listen, analyse and give guidance, lending a sympathetic ear where necessary but, in doing so, recognise the balance of the individual against running a commercial firm. Whilst one must strive to be fair and supportive, that must be balanced with strong leadership.

I am sure that my job is made easier because I have the added advantage of knowing personally every member of staff. Apart from building upon that relationship, I know that anything that is happening in the office will be brought to my attention by someone, if not the person/s concerned. However, some days can be taken up dealing with staffing issues – personal problems along with 'office' related problems – sometimes an ear is enough, other times serious action is required.

There is no great magic in performing my role – common sense and a sound practice philosophy make it much easier.

CASE STUDY   **Personnel manager (II)**

Human Resources – the new Personnel – is a very challenging role, no matter what position you hold in the department. Here we are a team of two, one being part-time, so there is lots of running around after 180 staff!!

Some people who contact you want your attention now and forget you have other work to do. You have to make them feel that they are the priority and take time to listen to what they have to say and deal with issues as and when they arise. Each individual reacts differently to problems and sometimes they feel they have a major issue to deal with yet when you talk about it you feel like saying 'just get on with it'!! Frustration usually kicks in when you get back and shut the door of your office.

An 'irritation' of the position is when you get people trying to be helpful and sort out something that they really know nothing about. When everything goes wrong they come to you to sort out the mess.

The feel-good factor kicks in when you end up spending time with an individual and you get a positive result at the end of it.

In summary it is a challenging but rewarding environment in which to work.

CASE STUDY   **Director of finance**

One of the main things that affects being an FD in a legal practice is the concept of 'Partnership'! For example:

- getting 20 or so partners to make a decision can be difficult, which is why you need to delegate management authority to a board and managing partner;

- at times of investment for the future, the partners revert to making their own personal investment decisions, dependent on their own circumstances, age, proximity to retirement, etc. I suggest this is human nature, although they insist they are making commercial decisions!

You also have to get used to the lawyer's 'way' when discussing an idea. This involves the lawyer playing devil's advocate and apparently disagreeing, until you think it's the worst idea you have ever had, then they turn round to say what a good idea it is and let's implement it!

On the financial management side, working in a law firm is not that much different from working in any other business. All the usual day-to-day financial management issues arise such as working capital management – including debtors, WIP and cash. The only issue is trying to persuade lawyers that although they all agree with the principles, it does also actually apply to them and their clients in the real world!

This type of appointment normally works well, and the comments above have a feel of roles that are functioning well. There are issues, but the basic concept of the job has been thought through and they have a clear brief.

Chief executives

The next stage of development beyond appointing professionals in charge of functional areas such as finance and marketing is to appoint a chief executive to run the firm. The appointment of such a person becomes a real issue in most firms when they reach perhaps 30 or more partners.

This is a major step, and so far at least, there are relatively few examples of it working well in practice. The problem is not so much finding the right person – although that can be difficult – but whether your partners are actually ready to hand control over to someone who is not a partner, and very probably also not a lawyer.

Many firms are simply not ready for this type of appointment, as illustrated by this comment from a chief executive shortly after being told her services were no longer required:

In communicating with the partnership I mostly found myself climbing a steep mountain carrying a huge pile of management strategies and ideas only to be met by an avalanche of opposing, traditional views coming down at a thunderous pace to bury me.

You need to be very clear about the role and the relationship of the chief executive to the partnership. Most chief executives will have their own ideas as to how this relationship could work, as illustrated in the following case study.

CASE STUDY   **Chief executive (I)**

I believe that a firm should be 'led' by the partners in a consensus-building approach, but not necessarily 'managed' that way.

They should agree a shared vision for the firm and strategies for how to get there – a good manager may assist with this, but should mainly be responsible for planning and making the strategy happen. If the equity partners agree/recognise this principle and let an understanding manager get on with the job, his/her ability will soon speak for itself, authority and respect will follow and hopefully a greater team effort between partners, managers and staff will emerge. The partners can then focus on clients, team leadership and external matters.

Contrary to my strong financial background, I find that the 'human assets' constitute the productive resources of a law firm and that is where my greatest time and effort is concentrated, not dazzling them with figures/numbers.

The former managing partner of one firm who had appointed a chief executive about a year previously stated very clearly that his partners had only reached the point in the past couple of years where they were ready to accept someone from outside. Over the previous four years the partners as a whole had been involved progressively less in management decisions, as more and more responsibility had been taken on by the managing partner and his team. They had therefore adjusted to not being actively involved. He felt that if that had not happened the attempt to introduce a chief executive would have been a disaster.

Even when the partners of a firm are ready to delegate authority, it can be difficult to get them to accept someone who is not a lawyer, as the following case study shows.

Chief executive (II)

My firm had the foresight to identify the fact that they did not have the expertise to undertake the wide range of management duties. They had also appreciated the impact those diversions had on their fee-earning capacity.

My role was a combination of the duties of practice manager and managing partner with routine access to partner's meetings. This had the makings of a challenging opportunity with scope for responsibility and decision making. Over the three years I have been there, however, the partners have appeared to find it difficult to respect the lines of demarcation, indicating an inability to accept non-solicitors on an equal basis.

Whilst a partnership requires cooperation, departmental lines are drawn and respected; however, in aspects of administration and management, those lines are often ignored and the delegation abandoned. The result can be confusion around the practice, duplication of effort, a waste of fee-earning time and a lack of job satisfaction for the manager who questions the level of trust being given by the partners.

Many people within the profession as a whole seem to have a view that a chief executive cannot take such high levels of responsibility and be devoted to the well-being of the practice if they do not have a financial stake in the business. Many candidates (including me) come from a government organisation where ownership is not an option but dedication is rarely questioned. That philosophy is therefore hard to understand and, at times, can be frustrating for many outside the profession.

Since creating the role commonly described as chief executive, the firm's organisation, staff management and, above all, finances have improved markedly proving that employing specialists can pay dividends. Partners clearly need to know what is going on around their practice but a chief executive needs the professional respect and freedom to carry out the role successfully.

It takes a change of culture and dedication to the change of approach to make full use of the new team member and keep the more able on board. It does, however, pay – literally.

It is essential, therefore, that the partners are ready and willing to give up aspects of control. It is also important to define the type of person you want and to recruit someone with the right skills.

Perhaps the most common background for chief executives to date has been accountancy. Such a person has the advantage of being accustomed to professional life, having served articles or a training contract, and having worked within a professional firm, albeit in a different discipline. Whilst no doubt having many strengths, not all accountants are good businesspeople, and certainly many lack the interpersonal skills needed to be a successful leader.

Other firms have consciously sought people with industrial or commercial backgrounds, retailing or the oil industry, so as to bring someone in with very different skills and past experience.

Recruiting professional managers

The key is to consider carefully what type of person you need and to take professional advice to help find the person. You should expect to advertise nationally for a finance, marketing, human resources director or a chief executive, in *The Times*, *Financial Times* or equivalent, and should budget for at least £30,000 recruitment costs. You should assume a salary equivalent to at least a salaried partner.

In the case study below Chris Denington, of Zinc Resourcing, who has recruited several professional managers for law firms, describes his experiences.

CASE STUDY | **Recruiting professional managers**

As a law firm develops and grows the partners will typically address the issue of internal systems by appointing an individual, variously described as 'practice manager', 'head of finance and administration', 'partnership secretary' and even 'chief executive', who will take responsibility for overseeing internal systems and policies, leaving the fee earners to focus on generating fees. There is great sense in this move. However, this person must add value to the partnership from day one and in my experience and for a variety of reasons, this is not always the case. Where it works the person appointed takes the initiative thereby ensuring that he or she becomes an integral part of the business; where it doesn't, he or she very quickly becomes a pariah.

Recruiting the right individual is challenging. Whilst technical competence is crucial, the individual must fit or complement the culture of the firm for there is no more difficult place to be in the world of work than a non-lawyer in a firm of lawyers. The real complexity for the recruiting firm lies in assessing whether the face will fit. To make an accurate assessment of an individual demands a comprehensive understanding of the role you are looking to fill.

To take the example of a practice manager, they need to be credible in the eyes of the firm and this credibility comes from understanding that the role is three-dimensional:

1. In the first dimension you, the partners in the business, need someone who can get on top of every aspect of the firm's accounting systems, policies and procedures, whilst also handling the day-to-day 'nitty gritty' of the financial and management accounting functions. But, in addition, if the gardener needs paying or the Health and Safety policy needs updating, your practice manager must be able, but more importantly willing, to sort it out.

2. In the second dimension your practice manager must be involved in matters relating to the strategic direction of the firm. It is not possible to be the custodian of effective internal systems whilst operating at arm's length from the partnership. All too often the link between strategy and implementation is ignored, leaving the practice manager to 'guess' at the partners' aspirations.

3. In the third dimension (and this is the most complex area to assess at interview), the practice manager must understand the 'political' dynamic in the organisation. No matter how large or small the business, the dynamic is there.

Any professional manager who feels that technical competence alone will carry the day shows a distinct lack of awareness of the demands of the professional practice. The implications of this for recruitment are significant. As an employer, ignore the third dimension and you will get it wrong.

SUMMARY

1.   As your firm develops and grows you should review its administrative support and ensure you employ an appropriate level of professional manager.

2.   Ensure you are clear what the role is and prepare a job description that is realistic and achievable.

3.   Do not even consider the possibility of a chief executive until your partners are ready. This is likely to mean that they will have had at least three or four years where decisions have been taken by a small management team, so the partners as a whole are used to not taking day-to-day decisions themselves.

4.   Take professional advice from a recruitment agency and be prepared to pay a reasonably high salary in order to secure a good person.

Note

1   ILCA, 146–8 Eltham Hill, Eltham, London SE9 5DX. Telephone: 020 8294 2887.

II

Understanding the figures

5

Understanding profitability

Partner earnings in England and Wales

There is a tremendous variation in the profitability of firms of solicitors in England and Wales, as indicated by Figure 5.1. This illustrates the net profit per equity partner by size of firm, categorised according to the number of solicitors in the firm.

The figure shows the median, and the upper and lower quartiles. The median is the middle value in the range and is not influenced by the extreme values (as the average is). The upper and lower quartiles indicate the range of values. Twenty-five per cent of firms are below the lower quartile and 25 per cent of firms are above the upper quartile.

The figure indicates an overall median profit per equity partner in England and Wales of £47,000. In a quarter of firms the equity partners earned under £27,000 each, and in a quarter they each earned over £75,000.

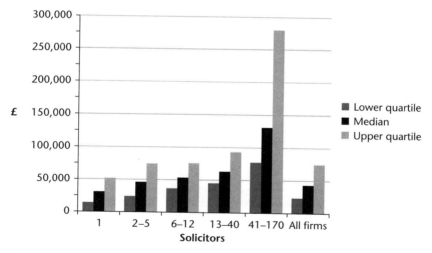

Figure 5.1   Profit per equity partner – England and Wales

Note: 'Net profit' is defined as total income less total expenditure and equates with the distributable profit as shown in a firm's accounts. 'Net profit per equity partner' is this total profit divided by the number of equity partners.

Source: The 2001 Business Survey, the Law Society

The smaller firms achieved lower levels of profitability, with single solicitor firms achieving a median of £33,000. A quarter of these single solicitor firms achieved profits of under £16,000. These are very small firms – many 'sole principals' have at least one other solicitor working with them. These firms, by contrast, simply have one partner, and on average also have half a fee earner and one and a half support staff. All the people in this category worked at least 30 hours a week on fee earning or management. A quarter of these firms had total fee income below £47,000.

The 2–5 solicitor group is more typical of the traditional small firm, with median fees of £300,000 and median profits per equity partner of £49,000. In this size group, a quarter of firms only made a profit per equity partner of under £27,000, which is still extremely low. Profits continue to increase through the 6–12 and 13–40 size groups, with median profits of £53,000 and £67,000 respectively.

The big jump takes place, however, amongst the larger firms with more than 40 solicitors. In this size group median profits are £126,000 with a quarter of firms achieving profits per partner of over £285,000.

Partner earnings in Scotland

Figure 5.2 summarises the profitability of firms in Scotland, and a similar pattern is illustrated.

The larger firms, those with more than 10 equity partners, achieved median profits of £139,000, and a quarter earned over £175,000. This group essentially comprises the large commercial firms in Edinburgh and Glasgow, as well as some of the larger practices in Aberdeen and Dundee.

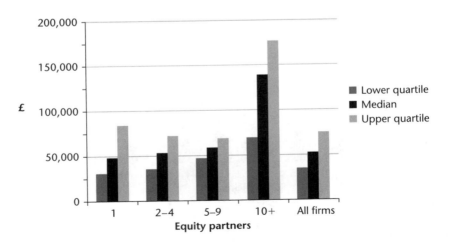

Figure 5.2 Profit per equity partner – Scotland
Source: The 2001 Survey of Law Firms in Scotland, the Law Society of Scotland

Interestingly, in the firms with fewer than 10 equity partners, some of the most profitable ones are sole principals, especially in rural areas. A quarter of this latter group achieved profits over £85,000. They earn high profits because it is often difficult recruiting solicitors in rural areas – they frequently prefer the cities – and the firms therefore have relatively low salary bills. There can also be quite good quality work available to these firms, such as inheritance tax advice for farmers. Some sole principals also work from home, and they often work very hard, sometimes to the detriment of their own health – but achieve good profits.

Median profits for sole principals are £47,000, with a quarter earning below £28,000 – very similar to firms south of the border. Those for 2–4 and 5–9 partner firms were £54,000 and £59,000 respectively.

Both of these surveys – the 2001 Business Survey in England and Wales, and the Law Society of Scotland survey – are based on relatively large samples and are therefore statistically representative of their jurisdictions.

Size of firm and profitability

Figures 5.1 and 5.2 indicate a split between the large, primarily commercial firms achieving median profits of £126,000 in England and Wales, and £139,000 in Scotland, and smaller practices.

Amongst the smaller firms profitability broadly increases with size of firm; however, you do not need to be larger to earn more money. Size alone does not bring greater profitability; indeed, as discussed above, some of the most profitable smaller firms in Scotland are sole principals.

You may decide your firm needs to be larger because of the type of work your partners want to develop, or because of your firm's market positioning; however, your firm's profitability is more likely to be determined by factors such as:

* the nature and type of your firm's client base – in particular whether you have regular clients or good sources of profitable repeat work;
* the quality and technical ability of your lawyers – and whether they are appropriate for the type of work your firm does;
* the type of work your firm does, and the extent to which it is offered by everyone else. The more you are able to develop areas of work which are, or are perceived as being, complex or specialised, the higher the fees you will be able to charge. When you are offering the same as everyone else in your town or high street you will tend, at least in part, to compete on price;
* the way the work is done, and who does it – in particular the extent to which your fee earners use technology effectively and whether matters are dealt with by appropriate levels of fee earner;

- the balance between publicly funded and private work – some areas of publicly funded work are poorly paid;
- the firm's financial structure – in particular its gearing, the number of non-partner fee earners you have;
- the willingness of your fee earners and staff to work hard.

The most profitable firms in both surveys will largely undertake commercial work, primarily for big corporate clients and institutions. They will have high levels of gearing and, generally, good financial structures.

The more profitable smaller firms in the two surveys are also likely to undertake a significant amount of commercial work; however, it is possible to achieve quite high levels of profitability from private clients, even legally aided work. Firms that concentrate on particular areas of work, do it in volume, and ensure it is carried out by the appropriate level of lawyer can also achieve relatively good results.

The LMS survey

Figure 5.3 illustrates the profit per partner achieved by the participants in the Financial Benchmarking Survey 2001 published by the Law Management Section (LMS).[1] The LMS has 1,500 members, 149 of which decided to participate in the survey. Although not representative of the profession as a whole, the firms in the LMS survey are more profitable than firms generally and are therefore a good peer group for comparison. The survey shows the same increase in profitability with size, and variation within each size group.

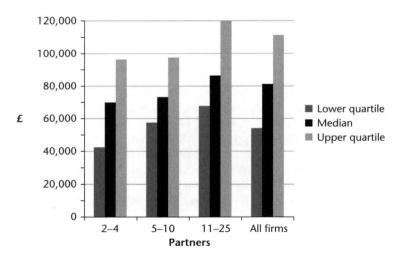

Figure 5.3   Profit per equity partner – LMS
Source: BDO Stoy Hayward/LMS Financial Benchmarking Survey 2001

In this survey firms are classified according to the number of partners they have – both equity and salaried. This survey contained a wide range of useful benchmarks and will therefore be referred to elsewhere in this part of the book. There were very few sole principals, or firms with more than 25 partners in the LMS survey, so these size groups are excluded from the charts.

Of the 149 firms, 16 were based in Greater London, 36 elsewhere in the South East and the rest elsewhere in England and Wales.

The overall median profits per equity partner were £82,000. The 2–4, 5–10 and 11–25 partner firms achieved median profits per equity partner of £71,000, £75,000 and £88,000, respectively.

Net profit percentage – the traditional measure

Traditionally, many (especially larger) firms assessed their financial performance according to the level of net profit percentage achieved, and 30 per cent was regarded as a good level.

This is simply the net profit available for the equity partners divided into the total fees of the firm. 'Net profit' includes interest earned on client accounts; however, 'total fees' is normally taken as fees excluding such interest.

If, for example, your firm's fees amounted to £2 million and you had also earned £100,000 in respect of interest and other income, the firm's total 'income' would be £2.1 million. If the firm's distributable profits were £650,000, its net profit percentage would be 32.5 per cent – i.e. 650,000 / 2,000,000 × 100 = 32.5 per cent.

Figure 5.4 analyses the 149 firms that participated in the LMS survey according to whether their profit per equity partner is: below the lower quartile; between the lower quartile and the median; between the median and upper quartile; or above the upper quartile.

The figure looks at the firms' net profit percentages and indicates that the most profitable still achieve around 30 per cent. There is, further, a fairly clear correlation between net profit percentage and profitability, with the least profitable achieving a net profit percentage of around 20 per cent.

Generally, the net profit percentage rises with profitability, but there are some firms where profit per partner is good yet net profit percentage is low, and vice versa.

Table 5.1, for example, illustrates two real firms. Firm 1 has recorded profits per partner of just £45,700, which is below the lower quartile for firms of its size, yet has achieved a high net profit percentage of 34 per cent. This firm has achieved a good net profit percentage primarily because it is 'top-heavy' with equity partners. The salaries bill is therefore reduced; however, once the profit of £320,000 is shared across the seven equity partners, the actual profitability becomes poor.

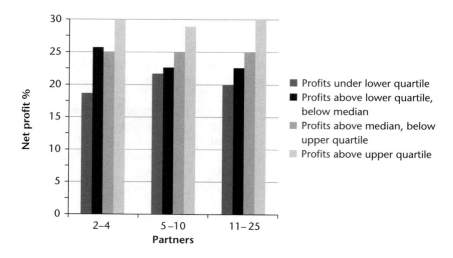

Figure 5.4   Net profit percentage – LMS
Source: BDO Stoy Hayward/LMS Financial Benchmarking Survey 2001

Table 5.1   Example firms

	Firm 1	Firm 2
Profit costs (£)	950,000	1,400,000
Net profit (£)	320,000	330,000
Net profit percentage	34%	24%
Number of equity partners	7	2
Profit per partner (£)	45,700	165,000

Firm 2, by contrast, has just two equity partners and, as most of its fee earners are employed solicitors, has a relatively high salaries bill and a low net profit percentage. Profit per equity partner, however, is good.

Instead of simply looking at the net profit percentage, firms should examine:

- the number of equity partners they have; and
- the level of net profit and gross fees per equity partner.

They should also try to get behind the headline figures and understand better the components of cost – salaries and overheads – and the relationship of these to fees.

The 40/30/30 rule

In order to achieve a 30 per cent net profit percentage, traditionally firms tried to contain salaries and overheads at 40 per cent and 30 per cent of their fees, respectively. 'Salaries' related to fee earners and staff and did not include anything in respect of the equity partners.

This measure was always flawed because, in excluding the equity partners, the firms were not making any allowance for their most expensive people! A better measure is to include a notional partner salary for each equity partner, in effect representing the cost of the partner as a fee earner.

The amount that should be included as a notional salary is normally equivalent to the salary paid to your highest paid fee earner. If you pay one of your salaried partners £75,000 that would be the figure to use. Provincial commercial firms could use £100,000. It is in effect the salary you would have to pay a suitably qualified solicitor to do the work of an equity partner.

An alternative is to use the same amounts as in one of the surveys. The advantage of this is that it becomes easier to compare your firm's financial performance to that of others. In the 2001 LMS survey, £60,000 was allowed for each equity partner for firms in London and £40,000 for firms elsewhere. The Law Society of Scotland used £42,125 for senior partners (aged 35 or over) and £37,450 for junior partners (aged 34 or under).

If these notional salaries were applied to the two firms in Table 5.1, new net profit percentages of 4 per cent and 18 per cent result, as illustrated in Table 5.2. This more realistically reflects the true profitability of the two firms.

Table 5.2   Example firms

	Firm 1	Firm 2
Profit costs (£)	950,000	1,400,000
Net profit (£)	320,000	330,000
Net profit percentage	34%	24%
Number of equity partners	7	2
Profit per partner (£)	45,700	165,000
Notional salary (assume £40,000 per equity partner)	280,000	80,000
Revised profit, after notional salaries	40,000	250,000
Revised net profit percentage	4	18

A good financial structure – the 40/30/30 rule updated

After applying a notional salary for each equity partner, the most profitable firms in the LMS survey – those achieving profits higher than the upper quartile – actually achieved a net profit percentage of 14–20 per cent as indicated in Table 5.3. The table also shows that the most successful firms achieved an overall profile of 50–55 per cent in respect of salaries and 28–33 per cent in respect of overheads. The 40/30/30 target financial profile therefore moves closer to 50/30/20 after notional salaries are included.

Table 5.3 also illustrates two other key benchmarks which are explored in more detail in the coming chapters – fees per equity partner and gearing (or leverage).

Table 5.3   Financial structure of the most profitable firms – LMS

| | Number of partners | | |
	2–4	5–10	11–25
Net profit as a % of fees (after a notional salary)	17%	14%	20%
Salaries as a % of gross fees	50%	54%	52%
Overheads as a % of gross fees	33%	32%	28%
Fees per equity partner – greater than	£431,000	£497,000	£639,000
Gearing (fee earners per equity partner)	3.8	4.6	4.1

Source: BDO Stoy Hayward/LMS Financial Benchmarking Survey 2001

SUMMARY

1.   There is tremendous variation in the profitability of firms, with a small group of large, highly profitable firms and a larger group of generally smaller firms that achieve much lower levels of profit.

2.   Profitability rises with size of firm; however, you do not need to be larger to make more money. You may decide your firm needs to be larger because of the type of work it wants to do, and its market positioning, but firm size does not of itself result in higher profits. There are some very profitable small firms around.

3.   The traditional measure of profitability is the net profit percentage; however, this is generally of less value today, and can yield misleading results unless a notional salary is used in respect of the equity partners.

Note

1   BDO Stoy Hayward/LMS Financial Benchmarking Survey 2001.

6

Fees, gearing and salaries

The previous chapter highlighted four interrelated factors that contribute to profitability – the level of fees per equity partner, a firm's gearing (or leverage) and its salary and overhead levels relative to fees. This chapter considers the first three of these in more detail, and the issue of overheads is considered in Chapter 7.

Fees per equity partner

It is perhaps fairly obvious that a firm's actual level of fees – the total gross fees as shown in its accounts – is going to have a big impact on its profitability. Higher fees in themselves do not result in better profits, but if the financial structure of the firm is right they can.

Some firms, in particular those that do legal aid, have worked hard in recent years to increase their top line fees but, because the additional work is often poorly paid, they have seen little improvement in their bottom line profits. The key is the relationship between the level of fees and the number of equity partners and, generally, the higher a firm's fees, as measured by its fee income per equity partner, the higher its profitability.

To illustrate how this is calculated: if you have eight equity partners each billing £100,000 and 16 other fee earners each billing £75,000, the total fee income of the firm is £2,000,000 and the fees per equity partner are £250,000. If there had only been eight other fee earners, total fee income would have been £1,400,000 and fees per equity partner £175,000.

Figure 6.1 demonstrates a very clear relationship between fee income per equity partner and profitability. This figure once again analyses the participants in the LMS survey according to their profitability and indicates a clear relationship between the two. It also illustrates the huge range in fees per equity partner between the most and least profitable firms.

The least profitable 2–4 partner firms in Figure 6.1 – those earning profits below the lower quartile, achieved fees of under £221,000 per equity partner. Those earning above the upper quartile, by contrast, recorded a figure of over £430,000. The difference is even greater for the 11–25 partner firms, where the equivalent range is from £300,000 to £640,000.

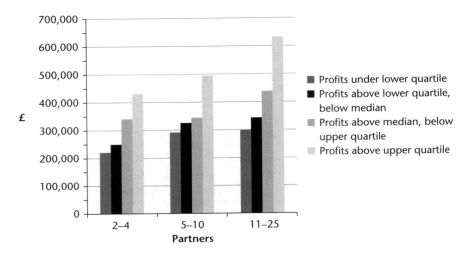

Figure 6.1   Gross fees per equity partner. (Note: 'Gross fees' comprises all income of the firm except income derived from the firm's investments and client accounts.)
Source: BDO Stoy Hayward/LMS Financial Benchmaking Survey 2001

The overall range of fees per equity partner for firms in England and Wales is shown in Figure 6.2. Two groups of firm emerge. The first group, comprising large practices with more than 40 solicitors, achieved median fees per equity partner greater than £680,000, and median total fees of £12.5 million, as illustrated in Table 6.1. The second group comprises the smaller firms with under 40 solicitors (which accounts for most of the profession), where firm size – as measured by total fee income – is much lower: around £80,000, £300,000, £900,000 and £2.4 million for 1, 2–5, 6–12 and 13–40 solicitor firms respectively.

Table 6.1   Total revenue and revenue per equity partner

| £'000 | Solicitors | | | | | |
	1	2–5	6–12	13–40	41–170	All firms
Total revenue (median)	83	301	925	2,411	12,474	325
Revenue per equity partner (lower quartile)	47	108	181	254	473	98
Revenue per equity partner (median)	83	167	262	397	680	171
Revenue per equity partner (upper quartile)	125	271	362	590	1,575	295
Median number of equity partners	1	2	3½	6	18	2

The 2001 Business Survey, the Law Society

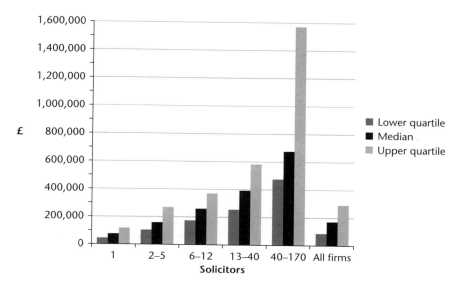

Figure 6.2 Total fee income per equity partner – England and Wales
Source: The 2001 Business Survey, the Law Society

Although these firms may be smaller in terms of total revenue, many compare well on the key measure of fees per equity partner. A quarter of 13–40 solicitor firms, for example, achieved fees per equity partner better than £590,000 – which is higher than a quarter of the 40+ solicitor firms. There is thus wide variation, with some firms doing much better than others and some smaller firms doing as well as much larger practices.

Figure 6.3 indicates a similar variation in Scotland – the larger firms performing significantly better as a group than smaller firms, but some small firms also doing very well. Interestingly, a quarter of sole principals in Scotland achieved better fees per partner than the larger 2–4 partner firms. These will include the most profitable sole principals.

Some of the larger firms, both in England and Wales and in Scotland, have developed new 'bulk' areas of work that are high volume but low margin. Typically these departments employ very few qualified lawyers, use considerable amounts of IT, and can generate significant profit – but at a low margin. If your firm does this type of work this measure has to be treated with some care. You may like to calculate a figure for the 'non-volume' area of the firm and compare that with the charts.

Fees per equity partner is therefore one of the key figures for any firm to examine. Firms that perform well may do so because their equity partners are high billers. It is more likely, however, that their performance is related to the number of fee earners they have in addition to each equity partner – their 'gearing' – and also the level of fees individual people bill. The latter will depend very much on the type of work they do, how hard they work and how good they are at billing.

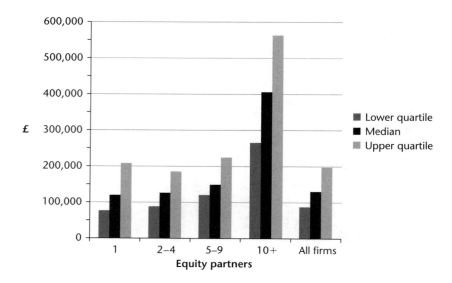

Figure 6.3   Total fee income per equity partner – Scotland
Source: The 2001 Survey of Law Firms in Scotland, the Law Society of Scotland

Gearing (or leverage)

Gearing – the ratio of fee earners (who are not equity partners) to equity partners – is an important component in the variation that exists in fees per equity partner and is central to the profitability of many firms.

There is a wide range between firms, as indicated in Figures 6.4 and 6.5. Figure 6.4, from the LMS survey of firms in England and Wales, indicates, for example, that a quarter of 5–10 partner firms had fewer than three fee earners in addition to each equity partner, but the highest quarter had over five and a half. There is a similar range for the other two size groups.

Figure 6.5 indicates that in Scotland, where the survey is more representative of the profession as a whole, the range is even greater. It shows that many small firms have hardly any other fee earners in addition to the equity partners, whereas others (in particular the larger firms in Edinburgh and Glasgow) have more than three and a half fee earners per equity partner.

In essence, it is generally difficult to achieve good profit levels if the equity partners are the main fee earners. There will be exceptions, for example niche firms where the partners are leaders in their fields and are able therefore to command high fees, but such firms are in the minority. In most cases profitability is better where there is good gearing, as illustrated by Figure 6.6, which once again analyses firms according to their profitability. The figure confirms that the most profitable firms in England

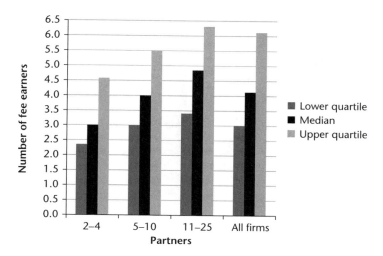

Figure 6.4   Number of fee earners per equity partner – LMS
Source: BDO Stoy Hayward/LMS Financial Benchmarking Survey 2001

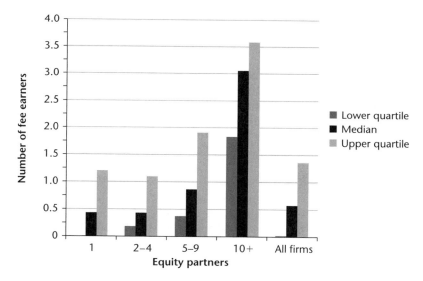

Figure 6.5   Number of fee earners per equity partner – Scotland
Source: The 2001 Survey of Law Firms in Scotland, the Law Society of Scotland

and Wales have a gearing level better than 3½ to 4 fee earners per equity partner. This means that if you have 10 partners your firm will have a further 35 to 40 fee earners.

The issue of gearing raises a wide range of questions concerning the type of work a firm does and who is going to do it. Good gearing is much easier to achieve in some departments or areas of work than others. The

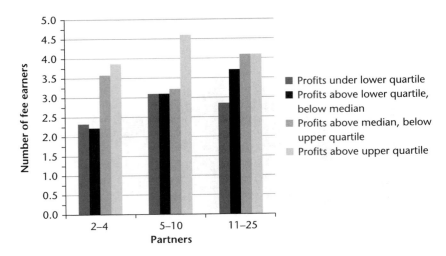

Figure 6.6 Number of fee earners per equity partner – LMS
Source: BDO Stoy Hayward/LMS Financial Benchmarking Survey 2001

bulk departments mentioned above can achieve almost unlimited gearing, with one equity partner running a department comprising a significant number of fee earners – but that is exceptional.

It also raises the key question of what actually is the role of an equity partner? A question many would rather not worry about! Is it to run files personally and to maximise their individual billing, or is it to run and manage a small team?

In the latter case a partner will still have some clients and will still spend part of their time on client work, but the actual work they do may well be different. Their cases may be more complex and they may spend more of their time supervising and training more junior fee earners. They may be responsible for a team generating fees of, say, £500,000 rather than simply a personal caseload of, say, £120,000.

When considering gearing, firms also need to examine their supervision standards and procedures because those with high gearing require a very different role and contribution on the part of the partners, managers and supervisors. It is not simply a question of employing additional fee earners and carrying on with a largely unchanged workload yourself. Invariably, the partners have to reduce their own caseloads to create more time for managing and supervising others.

This can be a strange experience, as the following comment shows:

> I moved from being my firm's highest earning fee earner to its biggest overhead when I stopped fee earning. The fees as a whole were higher, as were the profits, but my job had changed completely, and it took a while to adjust to it.

Quality standards such as Lexcel can assist in this respect because they require firms to consider both supervision and risk management, and require them to agree and document how these difficult areas are dealt with.

Improved gearing is something that may take a number of years to achieve. It can also appear to be a difficult goal, especially for small, 'general' firms where the partners are the main fee earners. If there are, for example, three equity partners and another two or three fee earners, and the firm does the full range of work typically found in a small town, it can be hard to achieve high levels of gearing.

The easiest way to tackle issues such as this is when updating the firm's business plan. How do the partners view the current position? Who is currently doing what? Are they happy with the status quo and does it generate acceptable levels of profit?

Some partners in recent years have concluded that they were not happy with how things were, and have set out to radically change their practices and the way work is done. Some have planned, for example, perhaps over a five-year period, to reduce their dependency on domestic conveyancing, and have seen it fall from over 60 per cent of fee income to under 30 per cent. Other firms have seen similar changes in other areas, especially personal injury, although often it was neither planned nor expected. The result has been a very different shape to the firm, sometimes accompanied by retirements or redundancies but also often by new recruitment.

Along with these changes many firms have also planned long-term adjustments to how work is staffed, and have thus improved their gearing over a period of perhaps three or five years. Others have concluded they cannot make real progress because of their relatively small size and have merged, creating larger units better able to achieve higher levels of gearing.

'Gross profit' – fees less salaries

A firm's net profit is determined by the profitability of its people – its gross profit – and the level of its non-salary overheads. The former is normally measured in terms of either a firm's salaries as a percentage of gross fees, or its gross profit (fees less salaries) as a percentage of gross fees.

In this calculation a notional salary is included for each of the equity partners, as discussed earlier, and the profit is divided into 'total fees'. This is normally taken as fees excluding interest earned on client account.

As discussed in Chapter 5, in the most profitable firms the salaries percentage is typically around 50–55 per cent; however, as Figure 6.7 illustrates, most firms do not approach this level. For half of the firms in the

LMS survey, their salaries were running at 60 per cent of their gross fees, and some were over 65 per cent.

In the most profitable firms, therefore, if the total salaries bill, including the equity partner notional salaries, was £1 million, total fees would be approximately £2 million. In the less profitable firms, where this percentage is about 57 per cent, total fees would be £1.8 million, and in the least profitable firms, with salaries at around 65 per cent fees, total fees would be £1.5 million.

These differences have a significant impact on profitability. Ten or 15 per cent of a firm's fee income is a significant amount of money and will account for much of the variation in net profit percentage and profit per equity partner. Firms wishing to increase profitability will find this is a good place to start because if this percentage can be improved it is likely the extra profit will translate into increased bottom line profit.

Fee-earner profitability

In order properly to understand a firm's gross profit it is necessary to look at the profitability of its fee earners.

The starting point for most firms (and in some cases the end point as well) is to look at the fees each person bills. The level of a fee earner's fees can generate feelings of great pride or deep dejection, depending on whether someone is doing well or not. It is almost a virility symbol in some firms – the big hitters are the driving force and the key to a firm's profitability. These people can be the most profitable, but this is often not the case.

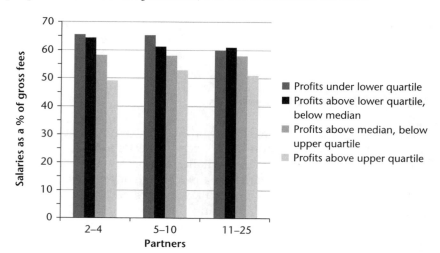

Figure 6.7   Salaries (including a notional salary) as a percentage of gross fees – LMS)
Source: BDO Stoy Hayward/LMS Financial Benchmarking Survey 2001

The main problems are that very often fee earners who achieve high personal fees – especially partners – need high levels of support staff in order to function! They also often run departments with poor gearing. The work is frequently technically complex, or perhaps they are simply poor delegators, but often high billers have few if any other fee earners working with them. By the time the cost of their secretaries, their share of a firm's overheads and their profit shares (which can be high) are taken into account, there is often little profit left. It is necessary to get behind the fees and look at the profitability of the work in order to understand the contribution of each department or team.

Historically most firms used to measure the profitability of their departments by allocating all their salaries and overheads across their various departments – and some still do. This has the advantage of reminding partners and fee earners of the total cost of running the firm, something they can all too easily forget. By allocating overheads, however, it is easy to achieve fairly meaningless departmental accounts that include lots of figures completely outside the control of the department head.

A better way is to measure profit after deduction of departmental salaries but before deduction of central salaries (accounts, reception, and so on) and non-salary overheads, as illustrated in Table 6.2. The table, which is for a fictitious firm, illustrates the type of format that could be used to analyse a practice's accounts. This firm is not doing well – departmental salary costs represent 59 per cent fees with a further 9 per cent being incurred on central salaries – 68 per cent in total.

Table 6.2 Example of departmental profitability, year ended 31 March 2002

£'000	Residential property	Family	PI	Crime	Total
Fees	721.6	335.0	569.2	290.0	1,915.8
Fee-earner salaries	225.0	35.2	61.5	177.7	499.4
Secretary salaries	237.5	58.8	22.5	25.3	344.1
Number of equity partners	2	1	4	0	7
Notional salaries*	80.0	40.0	160.0	0	280.0
Total	542.5	134.0	244.0	203.0	1,123.5
					59%
Departmental profit	179.1	201.0	325.2	87.0	792.3
	25%	60%	57%	30%	41%
Central salaries					180.0
					9%
Non-salary overheads					475.0
Interest on client account					−45.0
Net profit					182.3

* at £40,000 per equity partner

The table indicates that the family and personal injury (PI) departments are doing well. The family fees are entirely private and the PI work is all undertaken on a conditional fee basis. Residential property and crime – together accounting for £1 million fees, are far less profitable. This type of analysis could represent the first stage of a review to assess current levels of profitability and to highlight areas that need to be examined in more detail.

In the table, central salaries – reception and accounts – are shown as one figure and are not analysed, and neither are non-salary overheads. An exception could be certain overheads that are specific to a department, such as training, some library costs, and perhaps some marketing costs. Most of a firm's library and marketing costs would not be allocated because they are not specific. You would only allocate that part which is clearly identifiable to a department. Even some items which appear clear-cut can be debatable. For example, the property department may have run the seminar, but it was the employment team who won the new client! The principle is not to allocate overheads unless they are directly attributable to an area of work – the decision as to whether or not to incur the expenditure rests with the department head.

In the LMS survey it was possible to measure the profitability of firms at departmental level, as illustrated in Figure 6.8. The figure indicates that the most profitable firms manage to keep their departmental salaries to around 40–45 per cent, or, conversely, as indicated in Figure 6.9, they are achieving a departmental gross profit of nearly 60 per cent. This means that if the salaries of a department are £100,000 – including the fee

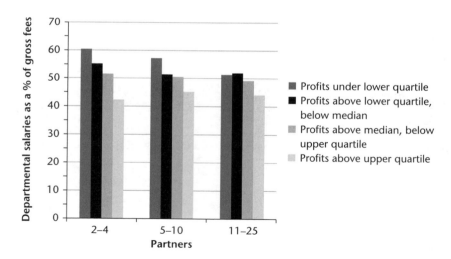

Figure 6.8   Departmental salaries (including a notional salary) as a percentage of gross fees – LMS
Source: BDO Stoy Hayward/LMS Financial Benchmarking Survey 2001

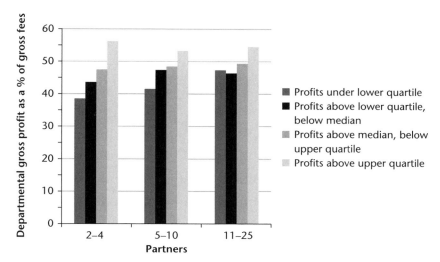

Figure 6.9   Departmental gross profit as a percentage of gross fees – LMS
Source: BDO Stoy Hayward/LMS Financial Benchmarking Survey 2001

earners and secretaries in the department and notional salary of any equity partners in the department, but excluding any share of central salaries – the department's fees would be £250,000. In the less profitable firms with departmental profit percentages of just 40 per cent, the department's fees would be £166,000.

Interestingly, there is a greater range in departmental profitability in smaller firms than in larger firms. This may reflect the greater significance of legal aid in smaller firms, or perhaps less sophisticated levels of financial management and control. Poor departmental profitability will have a big impact on the net profit percentage achieved, and this in turn will impact on profit per equity partner.

SUMMARY

1. Some of the most useful financial indicators for any firm are fees per equity partner, gearing and salaries as a percentage of gross fees.

2. There is a clear difference between the larger 40+ solicitor firms and those that are smaller, although some of the latter achieve very good results.

3. It can be very useful to analyse performance on a departmental basis – the most profitable firms achieve departmental profit percentages of around 60 per cent.

7

Overheads

The 'sieve' culture

Something strange often seems to happen to firms as they grow, especially during the transition from sole principal to partnership: money starts to leak from the firm in the same way water leaks from a sieve.

Sole principals are acutely aware they are spending their own money. If they decide to spend £500 attending a seminar in London they know their overheads will be £500 higher and their profits for the month £500 lower – not to mention the loss of fee-earning time. They are very aware of expenditure and are excellent at obtaining value for money. They are not necessarily 'tight' with their money, they merely want to spend it wisely.

Attitudes can be very different in partnerships, especially larger ones, where the feel of a direct link between spending money and profits can be lost. A partner once commented that spending money did not really matter as it was not his money that was being spent! It can even seem like a reinforcement of status, to see who has the largest office, newest laptop, best furniture or smartest car. In particular, as firms get larger they can become poor at obtaining value for money.

It is very easy to lose control and accountability in larger firms. The traditional approach of allocating overheads across departments referred to in the previous chapter does not help with this, often making it more difficult to get a true grasp on the firm's overheads. Firms with well controlled expenditure budgets and clear management accounts, in which figures are easily identified and understandable, have always been able to control overheads better.

Part of the task of effective financial management and control is therefore to reintroduce a sense of accountability and to plug some of the leakage in the sieve.

Process/investment related overheads

Non-salary overheads can be grouped into those areas of expenditure that are:

- **Process related** – such as rent and rates, stationery, telephone, professional indemnity, accommodation costs, library – they are *necessary* for the work to be processed;
- **Investment related** – such as training, IT and marketing. They are fundamental to the future development of the firm because they help identify new areas of work, improve the way work is processed, and improve the profitability of that work, but are *discretionary*.

The latter normally accounts for less than 15 per cent of fees, yet is often the first area to be cut in the event of any pressure on profits. Although many firms spend under two or three per cent of their fees on key areas such as training or marketing, these are often the first areas to be cut:

> I am not convinced we can easily increase our fees and believe we will have to look at reducing our overheads if we are to increase profits.

There is a great temptation to cut the wrong areas.

Process related overheads include many items that are relatively fixed, at least in the short term. Over time, however, it is often possible to obtain better value for money for these items especially if you introduce a culture of seeking value from all suppliers.

Whilst some overheads increase gradually, the larger items – an additional floor, a new IT system – tend to increase in significant steps. These steps can have a big impact on profitability and the challenge is to balance the level of a firm's long-term overheads with the number of fee earners it has, and the level of fees they generate.

A sole practitioner working from home and doing their own typing will have very low overheads – under £10,000 a year in low risk areas such as crime or mental health. Overheads will include stationery, telephone and fax, IT costs, professional indemnity, and so on. As soon as this person decides to rent an office their overheads will increase, perhaps to £25,000 a year, more if they decide to take on a secretary. As the firm continues to grow, so do its overheads, and a large city centre based practice can easily have overheads per fee earner in excess of £40,000.

Overheads as a percentage of gross fees, and per fee earner

Figure 7.1 indicates that most firms manage their overheads at around 30–33 per cent of gross fees, although some of the most profitable 11–25 partner firms are down at around 27 per cent. In the least profitable firms overheads are running at 35–40 per cent of gross fees. The high percent-

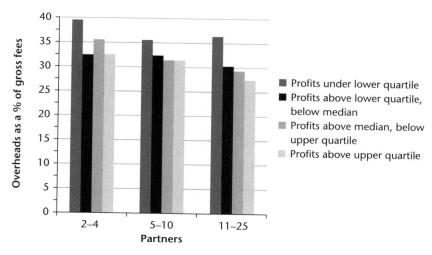

Figure 7.1   Overheads as a percentage of gross fees – LMS
Source: BDO Stoy Hayward/LMS Financial Benchmarking Survey 2001

ages in the less profitable firms could reflect high fixed property costs or may be due to the low levels of fees generated.

The more profitable firms are not necessarily spending less on overheads, but the level of their overheads can have a better relationship to the fees generated. Figure 7.2 divides the total overheads of a firm by the number of fee earners it has to provide a figure of total overheads per fee earner. This indicates that the more profitable firms actually spend more per fee earner than the less profitable firms. They are spending around £30,000–£35,000 per fee earner, as opposed to around £27,000.

This may be due to the type of work being undertaken. It is likely that the more profitable firms will do more better quality private client or commercial work and will occupy more expensive and prestigious offices than, for example, a small legal aid firm. They are likely to be in city centres and may wish to project a certain image and style to their clients.

For the firms in the LMS survey, approximately 21 per cent of their overheads were in respect of accommodation costs, 9 per cent in respect of IT, 5 per cent in respect of marketing, 2.5 per cent in respect of training, with the balance accounted for by all the other overheads of the firm.

Other surveys have indicated that around 35 per cent of a firm's overheads are attributable to accommodation costs, depreciation and professional indemnity. There is often little firms can do about this, in particular in the short term, therefore attention should concentrate on the balance, starting with the biggest items.

The comments of one of the contributors to *Cashflow and Improved Financial Management* (Otterburn 1998) – given in the following case study – still hold good in this regard.

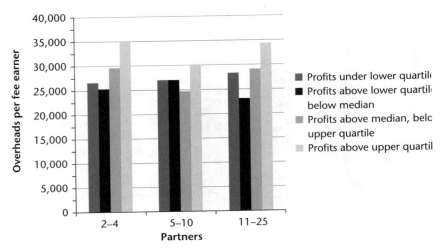

Figure 7.2 Overheads per fee earner – LMS
Source: BDO Stoy Hayward/LMS Financial Benchmarking Survey 2001

CASE STUDY **Control of overheads**

Many firms are poor at getting value for money from their suppliers. Often buying and ordering is left to the office junior who can easily have a 'junk mail mentality', and a tendency to overstock rather than risk running out. We are a four-partner firm with 38 staff and fee earners in total. We used to be very poor at buying, but in the last couple of years have become much better. We have taken advantage of the highly competitive state of the market and never buy any product without a competitive quote.

For example, we used to pay £2.40 a ream for A4 stationery. By careful shopping around we now buy stationery of the same quality for £1.50 a ream and, because we buy approximately 25 boxes a month, have achieved a saving of over £1,400 a year. We apply the same technique to all of our purchasing, including envelopes, notepads, counsel pads, etc. and overall have reduced our stationery budget by 20 per cent, from £28,000 to £22,000. A similar approach can be applied to other areas as well including furniture, computer hardware and insurance.

To sum up, our policy is:

• never sacrifice quality for price;

- never accept the first price quoted;
- always get at least three competitive quotes for any major purchase.

Above all, we get to know the market and the profit margins of our suppliers and we use this knowledge to our advantage.

The principles underlying effective control of overheads are therefore:

- to ensure you obtain value for money in all your purchases;
- to challenge all expenditure – why are we buying it?
- to challenge existing working practices and custom – why do we need so much floor space? Could we work open plan?
- to fix budgets in advance and allocate responsibility for the various expenditure headings so as to increase accountability.

The issue of allocation

Overheads are usually either specific to a department or are more general and relate to the whole firm. Examples of the former would include specific marketing, training or library costs. Examples of the latter would include the cost of the annual accounts, accommodation costs, depreciation and insurance.

It is good practice when preparing a budget to identify those items that are specific to a department and to allocate responsibility for them to the department head. They would in effect be given a budget for that item and would not need approval from anyone else for expenditure unless the budget was going to be exceeded.

Problems arise when attempts are made to allocate the firm-wide overheads across the various departments. At the end of the day, all the expenditure of a firm relates to the legal departments and it is relatively easy to argue that all costs should be allocated to the departments concerned. All that has to be done is to agree a formula for the allocation that is fair.

As discussed previously, most firms used to allocate overheads in their management accounts across their various departments or offices, and many firms still do this. They would base the allocation on a variety of methods, with the most common being on a per capita basis or pro rata to fees.

The advantage of this approach is that partners and fee earners are constantly reminded of the total overheads of the firm, but there are two main drawbacks. The first is that accountability is often reduced because overheads can be lost amongst the other costs of the departments. If overheads are spread across a number of departments it can be difficult to work out easily what the total is, and even more difficult to work out the amount on individual overhead items.

The second drawback is that the usefulness of the department's management accounts, as a tool to help departmental management, is very much reduced. Any real discussion about the performance of the department or team is confused by the inclusion of items outside the control of the department head.

As discussed in Chapter 6, overheads are better managed centrally and should not normally be arbitrarily allocated across departments. It is relatively easy to set a target amount of profit for each department that would cover its share of the firm's overheads and also its contribution to the firm's profits.

It can also be useful to remind fee earners of the total expenditure of the firm by calculating the salary and overhead costs each fee earner has to recover before they actually begin to contribute to the firm's profits. This is something any firm should be able to work out quickly, as illustrated in Table 7.1. You should include the salary of a two- to three-year qualified solicitor in your town, a typical secretary salary and the overheads per fee earner for your firm.

It is often useful to undertake this calculation on a departmental basis, and it should include averages appropriate for the department. Instead of a two- or three-year qualified solicitor, if the department mainly employs legal executives or paralegals, you should use a salary appropriate to them. Notional salaries should be included in respect of the cost of partners as fee earners.

Also, your fee earners might not have their own secretary. For example, crime departments typically do not have one secretary per fee earner and often a secretary can support three or four fee earners, in which case you should include the appropriate proportion of the cost of a secretary.

Table 7.1   Total cost of running a fee earner

	£
Solicitor salary (say)	25,000
Secretary salary (say) – assuming the fee earner has a secretary	18,000
Share of central staff (say)	5,000
	48,000
National Insurance (say, 12%)	5,800
	53,800
Overheads per fee earner (say)	27,000
Allowance for interest on partner capital and partner pension provision (say)	5,000
Total cost of running the fee earner	85,800

It is easy to calculate the overheads per fee earner for your firm, and this amount would normally be applied across the departments. It could be argued that some departments make more use of the firm's central resources than others, but there is a danger of over-complicating the calculation for little benefit. Perhaps the only significant allowance that could be made is for professional indemnity (PI) insurance. If your firm undertakes criminal work an argument could be made for charging the crime department a lower amount in respect of PI insurance – certainly crime-only firms have very low PI insurance premiums.

The calculation also includes an allowance for interest on partner capital and partner pension provision, and the latter has been calculated at 17.5 per cent of the appropriate notional salary. The former is an alternative to external funding from a bank and should therefore be included as a cost of financing the firm. The latter is a further cost to the firm that would have been paid to a salaried partner.

This illustration indicates that each fee earner needs to generate fees of £85,800 in order simply to cover their salary costs and share of the firm's overheads – a level some would struggle to achieve. If the fee earner was expected to produce fees of £100,000 this would generate a modest profit of just £15,000. Fees of £110,000 would produce a more worthwhile profit of £25,000.

Some firms apply a multiple to a fee earner's salary in order to calculate the minimum fees they are to bill. A multiple of ×3 salary has often been used. In this example, it is interesting to see that a multiple of ×4 is required in order simply to achieve fees of £100,000.

SUMMARY

1. Beware of a 'sieve' culture concerning expenditure and try to instil an attitude of accountability and responsibility.
2. Be aware of the distinction between overheads that are process related and those that are investment related. Be careful about unnecessarily cutting back on the latter.
3. Be determined to obtain value for money from all your suppliers.
4. Try to avoid allocating expenditure across the departments of the firm unless it is specific to that department.

8

Working capital

When trying to increase profitability, many senior and managing partners concentrate on the level of fees achieved each month and how they compare to target. Most partners and fee earners will be familiar with the year-end pressure to achieve budget, and the better managed firms will have a similar push at the end of each quarter or each month.

Whilst the level of fees billed is clearly important, a better way of increasing long-term profitability is to place greater emphasis on the control of working capital and how fee earners are actually processing their work. Firms that manage to reduce the amounts tied up in working capital have the potential to reap a number of benefits. These can include:

- a greater awareness of how each fee earner is managing their caseload, and what a 'reasonable' caseload is for different areas of work;
- a better focus on impediments in internal procedures and working practices to the smooth processing of work and of billing;
- better client care in terms of communicating the level of costs building up on a file and informing clients that a bill is to be sent;
- a better awareness of the cumulative level of disbursements and the need for client funding in advance;
- a better awareness of problem fee earners, problem clients and problem work types;
- a better focus of management time on the small number of matters or fee earners with problems rather than the large number of matters that go through smoothly.

'Working capital' comprises:

- work in progress (WIP)
- unpaid bills
- unbilled disbursements.

Most fee earners will be aware of the latter two items but relatively few will be fully aware of their WIP.

All firms now have to include WIP in their annual accounts; however, this is not the 'true' value of work in progress. The figure that is used in the annual accounts excludes the value of the time of the equity partners and will be based on very prudent assumptions – its main reason for inclusion is for the calculation of partner tax. Some small firms, where the equity partners are the main fee earners, will have very low WIP. If they are the only fee earners WIP will be zero.

The figure to be used in management accounts is normally extracted from the firm's computer system and comprises the time of all the fee earners. The printouts will invariably need cleaning up and often require a lot of effort before a reasonable figure is produced. This will be at selling price and will normally be reduced to cost.

Firms that are able to establish better control over their working capital get a twofold benefit. Perhaps the most obvious is that their cash position improves because they are able to reduce the amount of money tied up. The second, often less apparent benefit is that in order to reduce working capital you actually have to change fee earner working practices, and that has tremendous potential benefit for a firm.

WIP is invariably the largest component of working capital, yet it is the most difficult area. The starting point is an effective time-recording system.

Time recording

> My firm doesn't do it because we think (rightly or wrongly) that when fee earners cost their files they will be able to assess how much work they have done from memory.

There are three main reasons why all fee earners should record their time:

- billing
- management information
- information about the value of work done and WIP.

Traditionally most fee earners have regarded the main, or indeed, only purpose of time recording as an aid in preparing bills. Many view it as a complete waste of time, especially where they charge on a fixed fee basis, as in most residential conveyancing.

Arguably, however, the other two reasons listed above are just as important, and if fee earners do not record their time the useful information cannot be produced. It is especially important where fee earners are working on a conditional fee basis as it provides an indication of the potential value of future work.

Many fee earners dislike time recording, and it can in practice be difficult to do, especially where a fee earner has a large number of files. However, there is a wide variety of methods available, including traditional timesheets, light pens and bar code labels and direct entry via a fee-earner desktop. The key is to find the best method for the fee earners concerned and it is often good to involve them in that process, perhaps by arranging demonstrations of the different methods.

Some firms use time recording for billing and increasingly commercial clients ask for copies of the time-recording schedule to support their bills. Other firms automatically provide such reports to clients as a means of both differentiating their practice from others, and being more transparent in their billing. Firms that have full time recording are generally quite clear that their fees have increased as a result because less time is lost.

The discipline of recording your time almost always makes you use it more effectively. It makes you think about what you are doing.

Firms on full time recording are able to produce a range of management information such as:

- chargeable hours for each fee earner on a daily, weekly, monthly or annual basis;
- information on average hourly fees – by dividing the chargeable hours recorded into that person's fees;
- non-chargeable hours for each fee earner;
- an analysis of non-chargeable time;
- total value of work done each week or month;
- total value of WIP for each fee earner, team, department and for the firm.

Partners involved in management should not just be looking for poor performers, but also for those consistently working excessive hours. Most partners will probably work 10-hour days – 2,300 hours a year – which is not untypical of other self-employed people. But some will work 12-hour days, and will also come in at weekends, which is arguably not healthy or sustainable in the long term. If they time record you will be in a better position to know this.

Non-chargeable time recording is a great way of identifying poor working practices and inefficient use of time – time that could have been billed. In order to get a better grip on this area, one firm has produced a special non-chargeable timesheet. They already recorded their chargeable time but felt there were too few non-chargeable codes available. Their fee earners now have two timesheets – one for chargeable time, the other for non-chargeable time, as illustrated in Table 8.1.

The firm produces a monthly report of average daily chargeable and non-chargeable time per fee earner as a way of focusing people's minds on where their time is going. The calculation of average daily chargeable time is illustrated in Tables 8.2 and 8.3.

Chargeable time reports have to be interpreted with care. In particular, results can sometimes be distorted by the use of six-minute units.

Table 8.1   Non-chargeable timesheet

Fee earner.		Date. . . . .
	Units	Total units
Legal research (that cannot be charged)	1+2+1	4
Supervision/training		
Billing	2	2
Training/courses		
Franchising/procedures/precedents		
Marketing	3	3
Departmental meetings		
Firm-wide meetings		
Partner meetings		
Interruptions (1 unit)	1+1+1+1+1+1+1+1	8
Interruptions (4 units)	1+1	8
Interruptions (10 units)		
Administration	2+1+2	5
Other		
Total for day		**30**

Table 8.2   Calculation of average daily chargeable hours (June 2002)

	Chargeable hours per printout for month	Working days in month	Days ill/on holiday/on courses, etc.	Days at work	Average chargeable hours per day
Fee earner 1	135	20	1	19	7.1
Fee earner 2	95	20	3	17	5.6
Fee earner 3	125	20	0	20	6.3
Fee earner 4	110	20	1	19	5.8
Overall average					6.2

Table 8.3   Example monthly chargeable hours report, using the information from Table 8.2

	April	May	June	Average for quarter	July	etc.
Fee earner 1	6.5	6.9	7.1	6.8	6.9	
Fee earner 2	4.8	5.2	5.6	5.2	5.7	
Fee earner 3	5.5	5.8	6.3	5.9	6.5	
Fee earner 4	4.9	5.5	5.8	5.4	5.5	
	5.4	5.9	6.2	5.8	6.2	

Table 8.4   Weekly value of work done, June 2002

Fee earner	Chargeout rate £	Week 1 Hours	£	Week 2 Hours	£	Week 3 Hours	£	Week 4 Hours	£
1	155	20	3,100	36	5,580	38	5,890	41	6,355
2	125	22	2,750	24	3,000	28	3,500	21	2,625
3	125	32	4,000	25	3,125	36	4,500	32	4,000
4	90	22	1,980	27	2,430	32	2,880	29	2,610
			11,830		14,135		16,770		15,590

Some fee earners appear to have very high chargeable hours, but in fact have simply produced a large number of standard letters, and have been credited with six minutes in respect of each letter. This may be a particular issue within certain types of work, and care must therefore be taken in making comparisons. The comparison is more meaningful within each work type.

Also, some junior fee earners have low chargeable time because they deal with time-consuming tasks that free up more senior fee earners to generate higher fees. As always, therefore, the figures must not be viewed in isolation but in the context of the work the fee earner actually does.

The example in Tables 8.2 and 8.3 can be extended to provide reports showing the value of work done – on a monthly, or even weekly basis, as illustrated in Table 8.4. The value of the work actually done each week is very effectively illustrated by this report. This information is useful because of the gap that can occur between work being done, a bill being prepared, and the client actually paying. This is especially so in most areas of litigation.

Cashflow and Improved Financial Management (Otterburn 1998) included some useful ideas from individual firms on how time recording could be improved.

| CASE STUDY | **Firm 1** |

I started from the position that a number of fee earners were under-achieving both in terms of recorded time on files and in matching their daily six-minute units required of 75.

I developed a system whereby on a monthly basis I got a breakdown of the figures. Anybody who did not clock 75 units in a day automatically had this unrecorded time put into a special 'unrecorded time box'. In this way I was able to point out to people the amount of lost time they had each month and what this was potentially costing the firm in fees. I then talked to these fee earners about the way that they recorded their time and put them on a strict regime of properly recording time against a clock. The bad ones were losing £2,500 to £3,000 a month of chargeable time. The worst fee earners have now increased their billed work quite substantially and by nearly the amount that they were losing.

The most important thing to do is to make people understand the relationship between their target, the hours that it takes to achieve that target and the billable hours in a working day.

Why the Americans traditionally bill substantially more than the British is that they record more time. If an American lawyer lies in the bath for half an hour thinking about a client's problem the first thing he does when he gets to work is clock it on the computer, which I can bet you no English lawyer does.

CASE STUDY   **Firm 2**

An essential part of the billing process is setting up a manageable system for the accurate recording of time spent on specific files and the first decision that will have to be made is what unit of time will be used.

A 'unit' would normally be six minutes so that 10 units could equate to one hour. All time would be recorded on timesheets prepared by each fee earner on a daily basis. If the firm operates a computerised time-recording system the operator would then key into the computer the total time recorded against specific clients on a daily basis. The discipline of recording time takes a little while to acquire but very quickly becomes routine.

Most firms will decide that they want to have *all* time during the course of a working day recorded whether or not it is chargeable. Categories of non-chargeable time will have to be devised and will include such items as administration, courses, charitable work, holidays, marketing, etc. Any time not recorded in a specific category, whether chargeable or otherwise, could then be shown as miscellaneous time. Clearly this category should be used sparingly. In practice fee earners will probably find that they under-record rather than over-record time.

Whilst much work these days, and especially conveyancing, is done on fixed prices it is nevertheless still worthwhile recording time. A comparison between the fixed quote and the time recorded can be very illuminating. In some cases, this could result in certain types of work being abandoned or alternatively a reappraisal of who is doing such work.

CASE STUDY   **Firm 3**

We managed to save £5,000 by doing virtually nothing. This equates to £1,000 for each of the fee earners in my office. We have a somewhat elderly computer network but everyone has access to all features of time recording as well as the client accounts.

We used to record time in the traditional way by marking up a timesheet. We had a part-time clerk to enter the data to the computer system.

To save £5,000 the fee earners now type instead of write. It's not difficult! For £5,000 we would do it even if it was a bit difficult! The reality of the task is that there is no difference between handwriting the entry on a form and pressing the numbers on a keyboard. Most entries take no more than 20 key strokes. Further entries in the same ledger may only take three or four. With practice a complete entry only takes a few seconds.

The time clerk is instantly redundant but may be valuable elsewhere in the firm. Having the screen and keyboard on my desk means that all the firm's financial and time information is available throughout the day. This frees time for chargeable work. I do not have to keep bothering the cashier. This saves me time too. All the firm's management information is immediately to hand whenever I need it.

To summarise:

- All fee earners should time record. The discipline of having to complete a timesheet is of value to everyone.
- All fee earners should record both chargeable and non-chargeable time.
- You may use manual timesheets, but the range of options now available should mean you can find a method acceptable to most people.

- The main purpose of a time-recording system is to help identify the *cost* of a matter. It need not necessarily be used to determine the fee although it can help. It can also provide useful information in the event of a client challenging a bill.
- In some areas of work time recording may well result in increased fees.

Once a reliable time-recording system is in place it is also possible to calculate meaningful WIP reports for inclusion in the firm's management accounts. Table 8.5 illustrates how the value of WIP could be calculated at the end of the quarter. The starting point is the printouts from the firm's time-recording system, and these indicate total WIP of £440,000. Invariably these printouts are overstated and need to be reviewed by the fee earners to exclude any old or completed items.

There may also be matters where the time cost recorded exceeds the amount that can eventually be billed to the client. These cases need to be reduced to the value of the agreed bill, *less* the value of any further work to be done. For example, if a case is completed, the agreed fee is £1,000, and the value of time recorded to date is £1,200, the matter would be included at the agreed fee of £1,000. If the matter is not complete and a further £200 work is required to complete it, the matter would be valued at £800.

This 'cleaning-up' reduces the value of WIP to £332,800. A final adjustment is required to reduce it to cost – in this case resulting in a WIP valuation of £219,600. Because this is a time-consuming exercise most firms would only prepare management accounts with a WIP valuation at six-monthly, perhaps quarterly intervals.

Table 8.5   WIP as at 30 June 2002

Fee earner	Chargeout rate	*Per printouts* Hours in WIP at 30 June	WIP at selling price	Restated to exclude old/ completed matters	Restated at cost (less 34% for this firm)
	£		£	£	£
1	155	945	146,475	98,500	65,000
2	125	875	109,375	55,900	36,900
3	125	1,000	125,000	119,000	78,500
4	90	660	59,400	59,400	39,200
			440,250	332,800	219,600

Measuring working capital

As discussed above, working capital comprises WIP, unpaid bills and unbilled disbursements. The firms in the LMS survey had an average working capital ranging from £200,000 in the case of the 2–4 partner firms to £2,200,000 in respect of the 11–25 partner firms, as summarised in Table 8.6.

WIP is the most significant element of working capital, hence the importance of time recording and effective management of WIP. As discussed, the figure to be used is the true value of WIP rather than the value included in the annual accounts as the latter excludes partner time and may be unnecessarily prudent. In order to be meaningful it is necessary for all fee earners to time record.

Historically, unbilled disbursements have also been significant in many firms, and in some, especially those undertaking personal injury work for insurance companies or unions, they still are. Most firms, however, have become more businesslike at asking for payment in advance in respect of disbursements. Generally, firms have also become better in recent years at collecting unpaid bills, although some are very much better at this than others.

It is sometimes difficult to assess whether the overall working capital of a firm is high or low, and how it compares with other firms. Whilst of interest, the figures in Table 8.6 are absolute amounts and do not give any indication of efficiency.

The normal way of overcoming this difficulty is to relate the level of working capital to fees. The main measure used is that of 'lock up' – the number of days 'locked up' in WIP and unpaid bills (disbursements are not included in this calculation). A firm's lock up is found by dividing its daily average fees into the total of its outstanding profit costs (excluding VAT) and WIP, as illustrated in Table 8.7.

Table 8.8 summarises lock up for the firms in the LMS survey and indicates an average of around 128 days for the 2–4 partner firms, rising

Table 8.6 Working capital, median per firm – LMS

£'000	Disbursements[1]	Outstanding profit costs[2]	Work in progress[3]	Total
2–4 partners	17	67	124	208
5–10 partners	52	217	612	881
11–25 partners	113	556	1,565	2,234

BDO Stoy Hayward/LMS Financial Benchmarking Survey 2001
[1] Disbursements excluding VAT
[2] Debtors excluding disbursements and VAT
[3] WIP valued at selling price

Table 8.7   Lock up example

Fees:	£8,700,000
Fees per day:	£8,700,000/365 = £23,835
Debtors:	£1,757,000 (excluding VAT)
WIP:	£4,336,000
Lock up:	$\frac{£1,757,000 + £4,336,000}{£23,835} = 256$ days

Table 8.8   Number of days locked up in WIP and outstanding profit costs – LMS

Number of partners	Lower quartile	Median	Upper quartile
2–4	72	128	169
5–10	100	176	232
11–25	151	205	255

to 205 days for the 11–25 partner firms. The increase with size of firm is likely to reflect the extended credit taken by the commercial clients of the larger firms. It would not be uncommon for major plc clients to take three months to pay the bills of some of these firms. It is also possible that the larger firms are better at time recording than smaller practices. In particular, those doing residential conveyancing in some smaller firms do not use time recording and this will therefore result in an understated value for WIP.

Figure 8.1 relates lock up to profitability. Within each size group there is some correlation between higher profitability and a lower number of days 'locked up', but it is not clear-cut. The clearest correlation is amongst the 5–10 partner firms where the more profitable firms achieved lock up of around 150 days, compared to around 200 days for the less profitable practices.

As an alternative to lock up, some firms find it easier to relate their working capital to gross fees, as illustrated in Figure 8.2.

Taking the example in Table 8.7, this firm's working capital would come out at 70 per cent of fees:

Debtors and WIP   = £6,093,000
Fees   = £8,700,000
Calculation: £6,093,000/£8,700,000 × 100 = 70%

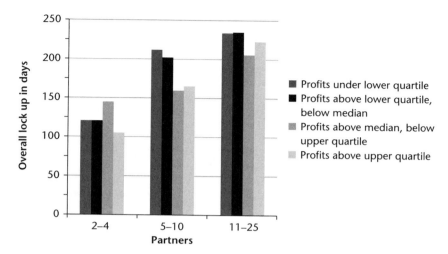

Figure 8.1 Number of days locked up in WIP and outstanding profit costs – LMS
Source: BDO Stoy Hayward/LMS Financial Benchmarking Survey 2001

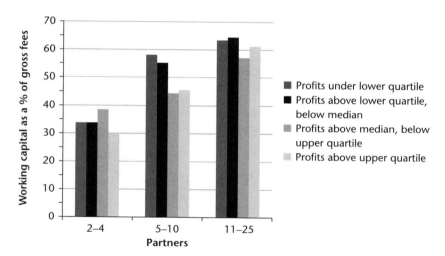

Figure 8.2 Working capital as a percentage of gross fees – LMS
Source: BDO Stoy Hayward/LMS Financial Benchmarking Survey 2001

Figure 8.2 relates the working capital percentage to profitability. To take the 5–10 partner firms once again, amongst the more profitable firms working capital is running at approximately 45 per cent of fees, compared to 55–60 per cent amongst the less profitable practices.

Reducing the level of unbilled disbursements and unpaid bills

Cashflow and Improved Financial Management (Otterburn 1998) included some useful ideas from individual firms on how they could reduce their levels of working capital.

CASE STUDY | **Firm 1**

Our disbursements used to be over £20,000, but are now always below £1,500 and typically stand at £650. We have eight and a half fee earners and undertake a broad mix of work, except criminal. Our general rule is not to pay any disbursements unless we have received payment.

We achieve this by the following simple controls:

*   In private work:
    *   disbursements may not be paid out of office account without a partner's prior approval. Normally there should be no reason why the client should not have paid us in advance or before payment is due;
    *   where the precise amount is not ascertainable in advance, we send the invoice/fee note to the client immediately and require payment within 14 days, e.g. counsel's fees or expert's fees (often we obtain estimates in advance and require payment on account).
*   For Civil Legal Aid:
    *   where the amount of the disbursements is known, we apply for prior payment on account if it exceeds £30 (disbursements may be obtained up to three months in advance);
    *   where the amount is not ascertainable in advance, we immediately apply for payment on account when the invoice/fee note is received and usually receive payment from the Legal Aid Board within 28 days;
    *   where the disbursement is less than £30 we apply for payment on account when the total of small disbursements exceeds £30 or, when

we apply for a large disbursement, we also include the small disbursements.

Our accounts department plays a key role in enforcing these systems. It is also easy to obtain payment from the client when clear written terms of business are issued at the outset.

CASE STUDY   **Firm 2**

My advice is:

- do not give an optimistic quote with which you will then be stuck. There is no point in buying work;
- always make it clear that the quote is on the basis that the matter proceeds smoothly and that if it does not you must reserve the right to negotiate a further fee or to revise your quote;
- mark the file on your computer so that you are warned when the initial time cost limit is reached and act upon it by contacting the client;
- interim bill in big probate matters, rendering a first bill no later than issue of Grant of Probate. At this stage one half of the value can reasonably be charged;
- be aware when interim billing not to charge more than the value of the work already done to date, even if the bill is only for half of the expected fee. Even if overall the total bills are fair and reasonable, if challenged each bill will be assessed individually and if it cannot be justified by the work carried out to that date will be reduced accordingly. You will not then be able to recoup lost work/charges on a subsequent bill;
- at the end of a job you may think 'I cannot possibly charge that'. You probably could have done if you had rendered interim bills.

CASE STUDY   **Firm 3**

Getting paid can be a real problem because:

- clients may not understand what we are charging for or how those charges are calculated;
- the client may not be happy with the service we provided;
- the client may not be able to pay . . . the list could go on.

However, these problems can be at least partially overcome if the client understands what your charges and costs are going to be. The following is a guide which should make it more likely that you are paid promptly:

- **Be specific**. Be prepared to be specific as to your charging rates and confirm that information in your client care letter.
- **Be accountable**. Be prepared to spend time in reviewing costs on an ongoing basis with your client, develop a practice of interim billing and be prepared to advise as to likely future costs.
- **Be clear**. Be prepared to explain your bill and consider attaching to it a concise and accurate breakdown of what the bill relates to. Be prepared at all times to discuss and explain your bill.

SUMMARY

1. Introduce simple systems that enable all fee earners to record their time. Investigate the wide range of methods now available and also explore the benefits of secretaries maintaining the timesheets rather than fee earners.
2. Make full use of the improved management information that will be available once all fee earners are accurately time recording, such as value of work done on a weekly basis and WIP valuation.
3. Monitor the amount of time lost as non-chargeable and assess whether this time could have been used more effectively.
4. Ensure effective systems are in place to minimise the amounts tied up in unpaid bills and unbilled disbursements.

9

Management reporting (I)

The director of finance or practice manager of a firm of solicitors should be a key part of the firm's management, helping the partners to understand the firm's finances. Good finance professionals will be self-financing through the improved working methods they should be able to introduce.

Some, however, seem to spend much of their time producing very detailed management accounts and financial reports that are:

- not really understood by the partners and lawyers reading them;
- produced in a format that is too technical and detailed to be of interest;
- over-concerned with the past, and insufficiently focused on what may happen in the future.

Many smaller firms, who do not have an in-house accountant, do not have the luxury of management accounts as such, and instead have to rely on extracting monthly or quarterly reports from their computer system. These are frequently too detailed and lengthy, and in providing every figure, fail to focus on what is actually important.

As with any other business, the success of a firm of solicitors very much depends on good, up-to-date and relevant financial information. This chapter outlines improvements firms can make to their basic financial reporting, and Chapter 10 goes on to consider how they can be improved through the introduction of work in progress to a firm's management accounts. It also considers the concept of the 'balanced scorecard'.

The value of comparison

The problem in many firms is that the basic layout of their management accounts is poor. They are difficult to understand and it is hard to pick out the important figures.

Table 9.1 illustrates a monthly accounts format many firms would use – in effect it is based on the format of the firm's annual accounts. Some of the problems with this layout are as follows:

- the figures are to the nearest pound, and are therefore difficult to read. Some firms even produce reports with figures to the nearest penny – an incomprehensible mass of figures – and many lawyers don't like numbers!
- by simply showing the current period and year to date it is very difficult to get any idea of trends;
- there is too much emphasis on overheads – 24 lines in this case – compared to just one line for income, and total overheads are, after eight months, almost exactly in line with budget.

Table 9.1   Smith & Co, monthly management accounts

Smith & Co: Accounts, Period 8, November 2002	This period		Year to date	
	Budget £	Actual £	Budget £	Actual £
Fees	250,000	235,458	2,000,000	1,850,478
Interest receivable	2,000	1,758	16,000	14,569
	252,000	**237,216**	**2,016,000**	**1,865,047**
Salaries	95,000	96,785	760,000	775,852
Rent and rates	12,500	12,658	100,000	102,457
Light and heat	3,000	2,480	24,000	18,456
Telephone	5,000	3,254	40,000	36,741
Printing, stationery	4,500	5,521	36,000	29,963
Postage and DX	2,000	2,321	16,000	16,879
Professional indemnity	6,000	6,000	48,000	48,000
Other insurance	1,800	1,700	14,400	13,789
Repairs	2,000	1,563	16,000	13,258
Accountancy	1,500	1,500	12,000	12,000
Subscriptions	2,000	1,850	16,000	14,785
Library	2,000	2,245	16,000	14,587
Training	2,000	2,203	16,000	14,695
Marketing	2,000	1,756	16,000	17,458
Depreciation	7,500	7,500	60,000	60,000
Bad debts	2,000	1,458	16,000	14,789
Cleaning	750	745	6,000	5,895
Miscellaneous	3,000	2,896	24,000	22,458
Negligence claims	4,000	2,147	32,000	26,789
Bank charges	1,500	1,452	12,000	11,478
Bank interest	2,000	2,851	16,000	17,452
Motor and travel	1,800	2,504	14,400	17,825
Annuities (previous partners)	3,000	3,000	24,000	24,000
Practising certificates	2,500	2,500	20,000	20,000
	169,350	168,889	1,354,800	1,349,606
Profit	82,650	68,327	661,200	515,441

A better approach is to make the information easier to understand in the following way:

- by simplifying the figures, for example instead of £235,458, make it 235.5 or 235;
- making the report landscape instead of portrait and showing previous months or quarters, so allowing better interpretation of trends;
- using charts wherever possible, because pictures are often easier to understand than numbers;
- focusing less on overheads and more on fees and the profitability of those fees;
- trying to highlight key figures and ratios;
- highlighting the items that are going wrong and need management attention rather than the items that are going smoothly.

Profit and loss

In the case of Smith & Co's accounts, there is really only one figure that is important – the fees are £150,000 below budget, and with just four months to go, profits are nearly 25 per cent below the level that had been hoped for.

Table 9.2 presents the same information in a very different format. These accounts are for November, which is midway through the third quarter. The first two quarters are shown in total and the actual results are shown for the first two months of this quarter together with a projection for December.

In this report less emphasis is placed on overheads – which are shown as just one line – and there is greater emphasis on the fees of the five departments. This highlights straightaway where the problems lie, and that some departments are actually ahead of budget.

Table 9.3 develops the format further and includes a notional salary for the equity partners. There are eight equity partners, and a notional salary of £40,000 has been used as in the LMS survey for firms outside London. The benchmarks in the earlier chapters in this book could be used to assess the firm's performance further. The table highlights the collapse in profits in the second quarter to just £42,000. The projection for December and also for the final quarter have been revised and show the effect of the reduction in staff levels that are to occur in December.

The purpose of this format is to present the information in such a way as to highlight trends and focus management attention on the key figures. It is intended to get people thinking about what is likely to happen in the future, as well as analysing the past. You may well decide you want additional columns showing the actual variance – the difference between the budget and the actual – or alternatively you may want to remove some of the detail. The key is to highlight the information that is important to you.

Table 9.2 Smith & Co, quarterly accounts (revised format)

Smith & Co £'000	Quarter 1 March–June		Quarter 2 July–September		Quarter 3 October–December					Month 8, November 2002		
					October	November	December	Total	Budget	Year to date	Full year projection	Full year original budget
	Budget	Actual	Budget	Actual	Actual	Actual	Revised	Revised	Original	Actual	Revised	Original
Company commercial	250	220	250	126	86	79	65	230	250	511	796	1,000
Property	150	140	150	125	41	38	35	114	150	344	479	600
Employment	50	60	50	55	18	21	20	59	50	154	224	200
Litigation	200	210	200	212	72	68	70	210	200	562	832	800
Private client	100	105	100	110	35	29	30	94	100	279	409	400
Total fees	**750**	**735**	**750**	**628**	**252**	**235**	**220**	**707**	**750**	**1,850**	**2,740**	**3,000**
Interest	6	7	6	5	1	2	2	5	6	15	22	24
	756	**742**	**756**	**633**	**253**	**237**	**222**	**712**	**756**	**1,865**	**2,762**	**3,024**
Salaries and overheads	507	492	507	511	177	169	150	496	507	1,349	1,949	2,028
Profit	249	250	249	122	76	68	72	216	249	516	813	996

Table 9.3 Smith & Co, quarterly accounts (revised format incorporating notional salaries)

Smith & Co £'000	Quarter 1 March–June Budget	Actual	Quarter 2 July–September Budget	Actual	Quarter 3 October–December October Actual	November Actual	December Revised	Total Revised	Budget Original	Month 8, November 2002 Year to date Actual	Full year projection Revised	Full year original budget Original
Company commercial	250	220	250	126	86	79	65	230	250	511	796	1,000
Property	150	140	150	125	41	38	35	114	150	344	479	600
Employment	50	60	50	55	18	21	20	59	50	154	224	200
Litigation	200	210	200	212	72	68	70	210	200	562	832	800
Private client	100	105	100	110	35	29	30	94	100	279	409	400
Total fees	**750**	**735**	**750**	**628**	**252**	**235**	**220**	**707**	**750**	**1,850**	**2,740**	**3,000**
Interest	6	7	6	5	1	2	2	5	6	15	22	24
	756	**742**	**756**	**633**	**253**	**237**	**222**	**712**	**756**	**1,865**	**2,762**	**3,024**
Salaries	285	289	285	291	99	97	75	271	285	776	1,076	1,140
Notional salary	80	80	80	80	27	27	26	80	80	214	320	320
	365	**369**	**365**	**371**	**126**	**124**	**101**	**351**	**365**	**990**	**1,396**	**1,460**
Gross profit	391	373	391	262	127	113	121	361	391	875	1,366	1,564
%	52	51	52	42	50	48	55	51	52	47	50	52
Overheads	222	203	222	220	78	72	75	225	222	573	873	888
Profit	169	170	169	42	49	41	46	136	169	302	493	676

Pro-formas

When designing new management reports it is always easier to have something to start with rather than a blank sheet of paper. An Excel spreadsheet with a number of pro-forma formats that you may find useful to copy and adapt is included on the disk that accompanies this book. The pro-formas are also included in this chapter, and are as follows:

- Fees
  - Table 9.4: fees by team;
  - Table 9.5: fees or average daily chargeable hours by fee earner;
- Management accounts
  - Table 9.6: quarterly accounts;
  - Table 9.7: overheads;
  - Table 9.8: balance sheet;
- Team reporting
  - Table 9.9: departmental or team report;
  - Table 9.10: departmental or team accounts;
  - Table 9.11: departmental or team summary;
  - Table 9.12: individual fee earner report;
  - Table 9.13: source of new matters;
- Cash control
  - Table 9.14: cash plan.

With the exception of the final document on cash flow, the pro-formas all follow a similar format and are intended to aid understanding by providing comparability. They have columns for each month followed by a total for the quarter. At the end of each quarter you may like to 'hide'[1] the individual columns for each month and just keep the totals for the quarter.

Certain reports use colour or shading to illustrate how they can be made more interesting, but most are simply unformatted tables.[2]

Fees

Two possible reports are included for fees. The first provides a breakdown by team or work type within each department, the second, an analysis by fee earner within each team. The latter must be treated with care. Traditionally this would be the one report every firm would produce and look at in detail; however, too much focus on individual fees can be counter-productive. It can result in partners hanging on to work they should pass on to more junior fee earners. It can also lead to fee earners in one team keeping work they should really pass on to colleagues in another team – or to another firm – because it is an area of law in which they lack expertise.

Table 9.4   Fees by team

Smith & Co   Fees by team

£'000	April	May	June	**Quarter 1**	July	August	September	**Quarter 2**	October	November	December	**Quarter 3**	January	February	March	**Quarter 4**	*Year to date*	*Budget to date*	*Last year to date*
Private client																			
Residential conveyancing			o					o				o			o		o		
Trust and Probate			o					o				o			o		o		
Financial services			o					o				o			o		o		
Commercial																			
Property			o					o				o			o		o		
Company commercial			o					o				o			o		o		
Employment			o					o				o			o		o		
Litigation																			
Commercial			o					o				o			o		o		
Family			o					o				o			o		o		
Personal injury			o					o				o			o		o		
Crime			o					o				o			o		o		
Immigration			o					o				o			o		o		
	o	o	o	o	o	o	o	o	o	o	o	o	o	o	o	o	o	o	o

Table 9.5   Fees/average daily chargeable hours by fee earner

Smith & Co
Fees by fee earner, litigation

£'000	April	May	June	Quarter 1	July	August	September	Quarter 2	October	November	December	Quarter 3	January	February	March	Quarter 4	Year to date	Budget to date	Last year to date
Commercial																			
Fee earner 1				o				o				o				o	o	o	o
Fee earner 2				o				o				o				o	o		
Fee earner 3				o				o				o				o	o		
Fee earner 4				o				o				o				o	o		
Fee earner 5				o				o				o				o	o		
Family																			
Fee earner 1				o				o				o				o	o		
Fee earner 2				o				o				o				o	o		
Fee earner 3				o				o				o				o	o		
Fee earner 4				o				o				o				o	o		
Fee earner 5				o				o				o				o	o		
Personal injury																			
Fee earner 1				o				o				o				o	o		
Fee earner 2				o				o				o				o	o		
Fee earner 3				o				o				o				o	o		
Fee earner 4				o				o				o				o	o		
Fee earner 5				o				o				o							
Crime																			
Fee earner 1				o				o				o				o	o		
Fee earner 2				o				o				o				o	o		
Fee earner 3				o				o				o				o	o		
Fee earner 4				o				o				o				o	o		
Fee earner 5				o				o				o				o	o	o	o
	o	o	o	o	o	o	o	o	o	o	o	o	o	o	o	o	o	o	

In large firms in particular, it can sometimes be very counter-productive to circulate individual fee figures to partners in other departments. There may be good reasons why a partner's fees are low – they are passing the work on to others in their team, concentrating on bringing the work in or managing the team. There may also be good reasons why a junior fee earner has low fees – they are taking on the 'rubbish', so freeing up others to achieve high fees. These points of detail, so important to understanding the figures, may not be apparent to people outside the department. Such figures must therefore be treated with care.

Management accounts

Table 9.6 provides an accounts format similar to the previous example in this chapter. There is provision for adding a notional salary and also separate lines for commissions and interest received. There is just one line for overheads and the detail is in Table 9.7.

Table 9.8 provides a pro-forma for a balance sheet – something many firms pay too little attention to in their management accounts. This includes a 'target' that the firm is aiming for at the year-end.

Team reporting

Tables 9.9 to 9.13 provide a series of possible team or departmental reports. Table 9.9 is particularly useful as it summarises a number of key figures on one page. This would normally be made available to all fee earners in the team, and could be used as a basis for discussion at a monthly team meeting.

Table 9.10 is a pro-forma for reporting team or departmental profitability. The key feature of this report is that it takes account of the salaries of the fee earners, secretarial staff and other support staff actually working in a department but not indirect staff such as accounts, reception or library. These are excluded and treated as a central overhead. Certain overheads are included, but only those specific to a department or team. All other overheads are treated as a central overhead.

Table 9.11 is designed to show movements in the working capital of each team and department over time, and also of new matters.

Table 9.12 provides key information for an individual fee earner. This is a relatively traditional layout and includes many useful figures. Its limitation, in common with many reports used by firms today, is that it does not highlight the exceptions that need action – it gives the fee earner everything and it is for them to decide which figures are acceptable, and which need action.

Table 9.13 provides an example of the type of report that could be used to analyse new matters by source. The key is to identify the types of source that are relevant to each department or team and to record as

Table 9.6 Quarterly accounts

Smith & Co	Quarterly accounts																		
£'000	April	May	June	Quarter 1	July	August	September	Quarter 2	October	November	December	Quarter 3	January	February	March	Quarter 4	Year to date	Budget to date	Last year to date
Gross fees																			
Private client			o	o	o			o	o			o	o			o	o		
Commercial			o	o	o			o	o			o	o			o	o		
Litigation			o	o	o			o	o			o	o			o	o		
Immigration			o	o	o			o	o			o	o			o	o		
Salaries	o	o	o	o	o	o	o	o	o	o	o	o	o	o	o	o	o	o	o
Notional salary			o	o	o			o	o			o	o			o	o		
Gross profit	o	o	o	o	o	o	o	o	o	o	o	o	o	o	o	o	o	o	o
%	o	o	o	o	o	o	o	o	o	o	o	o	o	o	o	o	o	o	o
Overheads																			
Overheads	o	o	o	o	o	o	o	o	o	o	o	o	o	o	o	o	o	o	o
Commission etc. received																			
Interest received																			
Net profit	o	o	o	o	o	o	o	o	o	o	o	o	o	o	o	o	o	o	o

Table 9.7   Overheads

Smith & Co   *Overheads*
£'000

	April	May	June	Quarter 1	July	August	September	Quarter 2	October	November	December	Quarter 3	January	February	March	Quarter 4	Year to date	Budget to date	Last year to date
Overhead line 1				0				0				0				0	0		
Overhead line 2				0				0				0				0	0		
Overhead line 3				0				0				0				0	0		
Overhead line 4				0				0				0				0	0		
Overhead line 5				0				0				0				0	0		
Overhead line 6				0				0				0				0	0		
Overhead line 7				0				0				0				0	0		
Overhead line 8				0				0				0				0	0		
Overhead line 9				0				0				0				0	0		
Overhead line 10				0				0				0				0	0		
Overhead line 11				0				0				0				0	0		
Overhead line 12				0				0				0				0	0		
Overhead line 13				0				0				0				0	0		
Overhead line 14				0				0				0				0	0		
Overhead line 15				0				0				0				0	0		
Overhead line 16				0				0				0				0	0		
Overhead line 17				0				0				0				0	0		
Overhead line 18				0				0				0				0	0		
Overhead line 19				0				0				0				0	0		
Overhead line 20				0				0				0				0	0		
Overhead line 21				0				0				0				0	0		
Overhead line 22				0				0				0				0	0		
Overhead line 23				0				0				0				0	0		
Overhead line 24				0				0				0				0	0		
Total	0	0	0	0	0	0	0	0	0	0	0	0	0	0	0	0	0	0	0

Table 9.8   Balance sheet

Smith & Co *£'000*	*Balance sheet* *Previous* *year end*	*Quarter 1*	*Quarter 2*	*Quarter 3*	*Quarter 4*	*Year end* *target*
Fixed assets						
Working capital						
Debtors						
Work in progress						
Unbilled disbusements						
	0	0	0	0	0	0
Bank						
Petty cash						
Prepayments						
	0	0	0	0	0	0
Creditors						
VAT						
PAYE						
Suppliers						
Accruals						
Overdraft						
Others						
	0	0	0	0	0	0
	0	0	0	0	0	0
Partner capital accounts						
Partner current accounts						
	0	0	0	0	0	0

much detail as possible in order to provide a genuine insight into where work is coming from.

Cash control

Table 9.14 provides a format some firms find useful in predicting their bank balance on a weekly basis. This is not the same as a medium-term cash forecast that may be produced for a bank. This could be shown to your bank, but it is intended as a very practical tool to help manage a firm's overdraft.

Table 9.9 Departmental or team report

Smith & Co   Team Report – Family

Fee earner	Fees £'000			Chargeable hours			Non-chargeable hours			Matters		Overdue debtors	Working capital		
	Week	Month to date	Year to date	Week	Month to date	Year to date	Week	Month to date	Year to date	Opened	Total open		Total debtors	WIP	Disbursements
Fee earner 1	0	0	0	0	0	0	0	0	0	0	0	0	0	0	0
Fee earner 2															
Fee earner 3															

Table 9.10   Departmental or team accounts

Smith & Co **Departmental accounts, Litigation**
£'000

	April	May	June	Quarter 1	July	August	September	Quarter 2	October	November	December	Quarter 3	January	February	March	Quarter 4	Year to date	Budget to date	Last year to date
Gross fees																			
Commercial		o		o		o	o	o		o		o		o		o	o		
Family		o		o		o	o	o		o		o		o		o	o		
Personal injury		o		o		o	o	o		o		o		o		o	o		
Crime		o		o		o	o	o		o		o		o		o	o		
	o	o	o	o	o	o	o	o	o	o	o	o	o	o	o	o	o	o	o
Departmental salaries		o		o		o	o	o		o		o		o		o	o		
Notional salary		o		o		o	o	o		o		o		o		o	o		
Gross profit	o	o	o	o	o	o	o	o	o	o	o	o	o	o	o	o	o	o	o
%	o	o	o	o	o	o	o	o	o	o	o	o	o	o	o	o	o	o	o
Overheads (department specific):																			
Marketing																			
Training		o		o		o	o	o		o		o		o		o	o	o	o
Library		o		o		o	o	o		o		o		o		o	o	o	o
etc.																			
Departmental profit	o	o	o	o	o	o	o	o	o	o	o	o	o	o	o	o	o	o	o

Table 9.11 Departmental or team summary

Smith & Co																		
Departmental report, Litigation																		
Fees £'000	*April*	*May*	*June*	*Quarter 1*	*July*	*August*	*September*	*Quarter 2*	*October*	*November*	*December*	*Quarter 3*	*January*	*February*	*March*	*Quarter 4*	*Year to date*	*Budget to date*	*Last year to date*
Private client																		
Commercial																		
Litigation																		
Immigration	0	0	0	0	0	0	0	0	0	0	0	0	0	0	0	0	0	0

New matters	*April*	*May*	*June*	*Quarter 1*	*July*	*August*	*September*	*Quarter 2*	*October*	*November*	*December*	*Quarter 3*	*January*	*February*	*March*	*Quarter 4*	*Year to date*	*Budget to date*	*Last year to date*
Private client																		
Commercial																		
Litigation																		
Immigration	0	0	0	0	0	0	0	0	0	0	0	0	0	0	0	0	0	0

Disbursements	*April*	*May*	*June*	*July*	*August*	*September*	*October*	*November*	*December*	*January*	*February*	*March*
Private client												
Commercial												
Litigation												
Immigration	0	0	0	0	0	0	0	0	0	0	0	0

Table 9.12   Individual fee earner report

	Month		Year to date	
	Actual	*Target*	*Actual*	*Target*
Matters				
Opened				
Closed				
Currently open				
Fees billed				
Recovery %				
Time				
Chargeable hours				
Chargeable hours per day				
Non-chargeable hours				
Non-chargeable hours per day				
WIP				
Chargeable time value £				
Unbilled WIP £				
Outstanding bills				
0–30 days				
30–60 days				
Over 60 days				
Total				
Unbilled disbursements				

Using information to motivate people

As well as reviewing the format of your firm's management and financial reporting, you should spend some time considering what information is shown to your equity partners, salaried partners, fee earners and staff.

Traditionally, most firms have been extremely secretive about any financial information, and many still are. If, however, you wish to motivate people and obtain the best from them, one of the most effective techniques is to involve them more so they understand better what is going on.

Most people are interested in knowing how they and their firm are doing, and if they have this information they often work better and are more effective at their work. It also increases loyalty and helps in staff retention – especially at assistant solicitor level.

Some of the firms who have particular problems retaining their better solicitors are those that insist on keeping them in the dark and treating them as fee-earning machines. Such a relationship becomes purely commercial – you pay them a salary in return for processing an ever-greater volume of files. They get bored and in due course leave for a

Table 9.13 Source of new matters

Smith & Co
Source of new matters

£'000	April	May	June	Quarter 1	July	August	September	Quarter 2	October	November	December	Quarter 3	January	February	March	Quarter 4	Year to date	Budget to date	Last year to date
Private client																			
Existing clients				o				o				o				o	o		
Estate agents				o				o				o				o	o		
Banks				o				o				o				o	o		
Building societies				o				o				o				o	o		
Yellow Pages				o				o				o				o	o		
Casual				o				o				o				o	o		
etc. . .				o				o				o				o	o		
Commercial																			
Existing clients				o				o				o				o	o		
PWC				o				o				o				o	o		
Grant Thornton				o				o				o				o	o		
PKF				o				o				o				o	o		
NatWest				o				o				o				o	o		
Barclays				o				o				o				o	o		
etc. . .				o				o				o				o	o		
Litigation																			
Existing clients				o				o				o				o	o		
Duty solicitor				o				o				o				o	o		
Other solicitors				o				o				o				o	o		
Accident Line				o				o				o				o	o		
Claims Direct				o				o				o				o	o		
CAB				o				o				o				o	o		
etc. . .				o				o				o				o	o		
Immigration																			
Existing clients				o				o				o				o	o		
Other solicitors				o				o				o				o	o		
Indian High Commission				o				o				o				o	o		
etc. . .				o				o				o				o	o		
	o	o	o	o	o	o	o	o	o	o	o	o	o	o	o	o	o	o	o

Table 9.14 Cash plan

Smith & Co   *Cash Plan*

£'000	W/C:...... Plan	Actual	W/C:...... Plan	Actual	W/C:...... Plan	Actual	W/C:...... Plan	Actual	W/C:...... Plan	Actual	W/C:...... Plan	Actual	W/C:...... Plan	Actual	W/C:...... Plan	Actual	W/C:...... Plan	Actual	W/C:...... Plan	Actual	W/C:...... Plan	Actual	W/C:...... Plan	Actual
Payments																								
Salaries																								
PAYE																								
VAT																								
Rent																								
Standing orders																								
Income tax																								
Drawings																								
Other																								
Total payments	0	0	0	0	0	0	0	0	0	0	0	0	0	0	0	0	0	0	0	0	0	0	0	0
Receipts																								
LSC standard monthly payment (Civil)																								
LSC standard monthly payment (Crime)																								
Significant client balances:																								
Misc. smaller receipts																								
Total receipts	0	0	0	0	0	0	0	0	0	0	0	0	0	0	0	0	0	0	0	0	0	0	0	0
Net In/(out)	0	0	0	0	0	0	0	0	0	0	0	0	0	0	0	0	0	0	0	0	0	0	0	0
Balance B/F																								
Balance C/F																								

higher salary. Those firms that are better at retaining key people are those that make them feel more involved. They don't just tell them what their individual fee targets are, they give them the fee budget for the whole team, or the whole firm, and they let them have monthly or quarterly reports monitoring progress against budget. They may also give them information about the profitability of their team, the level of unbilled disbursements, and what the overdraft is. These are key figures that give people a feel for how the firm is doing.

Secretaries and other support staff are also interested in knowing overall how the firm is doing. They may not want or understand the detail, but they are interested in the headline figures.

Some firms may be concerned that more information will cause their staff to ask for additional salary increases. Others take the view that if their staff are more motivated they work more effectively and that they would be prepared to share some of those additional profits through higher salaries, or perhaps a bonus. In other instances, staff have assumed their firm is actually doing much better than it is – in the absence of any information, and faced with a wall of secrecy staff draw their own conclusions!

Time should also be spent thinking about how the information will be used, and how it will be received. There is a big difference between firms that use information to put pressure on people and in some cases to humiliate them, and those that try to use it to motivate. It comes down to the culture of the firm and the style of the individual partners and managers.

SUMMARY

1.   You should critically review the format of the financial information your firm produces to ensure it is easy to understand and highlights key figures.
2.   Be imaginative in your use of charts and graphs as pictures are often easier to understand than figures.
3.   Make full use of tools such as Excel to produce simple reports tailored to your firm.
4.   Be prepared to share financial information with fee earners because they normally perform better if they understand how they – and the firm – are doing.

Notes

1   Using Format, Column, Hide.
2   The appearance of a report in Excel can be improved by using Format, AutoFormat.

10

Management reporting (II)

Chapter 9 provided some ideas on a better format of management information that can be of great help in the running of a successful firm. The emphasis was on trying to identify key figures and trends, and making the information easier for partners and fee earners to understand. Although hopefully clearer, these formats are still relatively traditional.

The main limitation with the management accounts of most firms of solicitors is that they do not take account of work in progress, and that can have a significant impact on a quarter's results. The next stage, therefore, in the process of making a firm's management information more useful is to include WIP.

In recent years there has also been much discussion amongst accountants, in particular those in industry, about the value of traditional management accounts, and alternative ideas have evolved around the 'balanced scorecard' concept.

This chapter considers both of these areas.

Work in progress in management accounts

As discussed in Chapter 8, the first point to emphasise is that work in progress is not the same figure that would normally appear in a firm's annual accounts. The latter excludes any time in respect of the equity partners and will normally be a very prudent calculation. Equity partners are excluded because there is no cost for them in the accounts – they receive a share of the firm's profits – and it would therefore be incorrect to include their time in work in progress.

Work in progress in a firm's management accounts will be based on the work of all fee earners, including the equity partners, and the starting point will be the firm's WIP printouts. As illustrated in Chapter 8, in most cases these are likely to require considerable manual adjustment and checking before a reasonably reliable figure can be obtained.

WIP printouts are usually valued at selling price and normally these would be reduced to 'cost' for inclusion in the management accounts. WIP is reduced to cost so as to avoid taking the profit on the work into the accounts until the matter is finished.

Some firms keep the value of WIP at selling price in their management accounts, although this is unusual. The great advantage of valuing WIP at selling price in the management accounts is that it is much easier for partners and fee earners to understand. The problem is that unless a subsequent adjustment is made to reduce WIP to cost, profits will be overstated and will not agree to the annual accounts.

Incorporating WIP: a simple example

The use of WIP is best illustrated by a simple example. This is for a firm with three departments, and Table 10.1 shows the initial accounts for the departments before WIP is included.

The commercial department is the most profitable of the three in terms of both the amount of profit generated and as a percentage of fees. In particular, it is much more profitable than the family department – with similar fees, the commercial department generated a profit of £155,000 compared to just £94,000 for family.

The fee earners have checked their printouts at both 30 June and 30 September, and the total value of 'clean' WIP at selling price is £1.2 million and £1.1 million respectively. In order to reduce this to cost it has been reduced by 25 per cent as illustrated in Table 10.2.

The opening and closing WIP, at cost, is then brought into the accounts, as illustrated in Table 10.3. Now that WIP has been included a different pattern of profitability emerges.

The commercial department has seen its WIP fall from £465,000 to £349,000. The effect of this is to increase the department's 'cost of sales' – the cost of doing the quarter's work, and its high profit has been reduced to just £39,000.

The family department, by contrast, has seen its WIP increase – by over £40,000 – and this is translated into higher profits of £135,000. The

Table 10.1   Management accounts, three months to 30 September 2002

£'000	Commercial	Family	Property	Total
Fees for quarter	279.0	273.0	231.2	783.2
Dept. salaries				
Fee earners	47.9	78.4	58.8	185.1
Secretaries	45.4	60.5	30.2	136.1
Equity partner notional	30.0	40.0	30.0	100.0
Total	123.3	178.9	119.0	421.2
Dept. profit	155.7	94.1	112.2	362.0
Percentage	56%	34%	48%	46%

Table 10.2 WIP valuation as at 30 September 2002

£'000	Commercial	Family	Property	Total
Opening WIP (1 July):				
at selling price	621.0	457.0	152.0	1,230.0
at cost (75%)	**465.8**	**342.8**	**114.0**	**922.6**
Opening WIP (30 September):				
at selling price	466.8	512.0	145.0	1,123.8
at cost (75%)	**349.4**	**384.0**	**108.9**	**842.3**

Note: 75% is not necessarily a typical percentage – each firm needs to calculate an appropriate figure.

Table 10.3 Management accounts, three months to 30 September 2002 with WIP

£'000	Commercial	Family	Property	Total
Fees for quarter	279.0	273.0	231.2	783.2
Opening WIP (1 July)	**465.8**	**342.8**	**114.0**	**922.6**
Dept. salaries	**123.3**	**178.9**	**119.0**	**421.2**
Closing WIP (30 September)	−349.4	−384.0	−108.9	−842.3
Cost of sales	239.7	137.7	124.1	501.5
Dept. profit	39.3	135.3	107.1	281.7
Percentage	14%	49%	46%	36%

property department saw little change in WIP levels and therefore unchanged profits.

This illustration, albeit simple, demonstrates the much better understanding that results from the inclusion of WIP in a firm's management accounts. It is quite likely that if the firm did not include WIP in its accounts, no one would have really been aware of the true position. The accounts in Table 10.1 show a strong performance by the commercial department, and although the partners in that department will be aware that work levels had fallen, they will probably not have fully appreciated how bad the position was. It would only be during the next quarter, to 31 December, that the other partners may have realised that there was a problem as the fees billed reduced. That would have been four or five months after the problem arose.

An alternative way of dealing with WIP is to bring it into the firm's management accounts at selling value and to calculate the value of work done, as illustrated in Table 10.4.

The effect of including WIP at selling price is to magnify the impact of movements in WIP. The commercial department is now showing a

Table 10.4   Management accounts, three months to 30 September 2002 with WIP, at selling value (SV)

£'000	Commercial	Family	Property	Total
Fees for quarter	279.0	273.0	231.2	783.2
less WIP at 1 July (at SV)	−621.0	−457.0	−152.0	−1,230.0
add WIP at 30 September (at SV)	466.8	512.0	145.0	1,123.8
Sales value of work done	**124.8**	**328.0**	**224.2**	**677.0**
Dept. salaries	**123.3**	**178.9**	**119.0**	**421.2**
Dept. profit	1.5	149.1	105.2	255.8
Percentage	1%	45%	47%	38%

profit of just £1,500, and the family department profit has increased to £149,000. Firms that produce their accounts on this basis, with WIP included at selling price, generally agree that they are much easier for people to understand. In particular, it would be relatively easy to provide each fee earner with a copy of the accounts shown in Table 10.4 – either for all three departments, or just for their department – together with an analysis of fees and WIP by team or fee earner.

Where WIP is valued at selling price it would be prudent to make an adjustment in the management accounts to take out the profit element of work in progress.

Overall, therefore, the inclusion of WIP in the management accounts of a firm greatly increases their value as a management tool. In practice this is probably best done on a quarterly basis and the figures should be analysed by department. Most firms would include WIP at cost, but perhaps you could try both methods and see which is most useful for you.

Balanced scorecards

For some years there has been growing debate within the accountancy profession, in particular amongst those in industry, as to the value of traditional financial reporting. The principal criticisms have been that management reports:

- can be difficult for anyone other than accountants to understand properly;
- provide far too much detail;
- do not highlight the figures that need action;
- tend to report only financial information, in part because this can be easily measured – whereas this is only part of the story.

A solution that is in the early stages of being introduced in law firms is the concept of the 'balanced scorecard'. The scorecards are 'balanced' in the sense that they include non-financial measures of performance. These might include:

- Marketing statistics:
  - number of new instructions
  - number of articles published
  - number of contact/client marketing events;
- Staff and personal development:
  - trainee supervision hours achieved
  - staff turnover
  - overtime hours worked;
- Know-how and research:
  - number of articles contributed to know-how database
  - hours recorded updating database
  - hours recorded training other fee earners on particular aspects of database;
- Personal:
  - number of days holiday
  - number of days ill
  - number of continuing professional development (CPD) hours achieved.

The objective would be to set an annual benchmark in respect of each area, such as:

- number of CPD hours for each fee earner – say, 20 a year;
- number of articles to be written by each fee earner – say, three a year;
- number of seminars to be delivered by each fee earner – say, one a year;
- number of days holiday – say, 25 a year.

When the areas to be reported against are established, a simple one-page report is designed and a 'traffic light' system is used to indicate areas that require action:

- red box = needs action;
- amber box = within 10 per cent of budget;
- green box = OK.

Curiously it appears to be the IT suppliers, rather than the accountants, that are taking the lead in the introduction of this type of reporting, and two companies, Elite and Norwel, are amongst the market leaders.

Figure 10.1 illustrates a scorecard. Technically, this is not a balanced scorecard in that it just deals with financial issues, but it provides a good example of what can be achieved. It was developed by Manchester law

Figure 10.1 Balanced scorecard (courtesy of Cobbetts Solicitors, Manchester and Norwel)

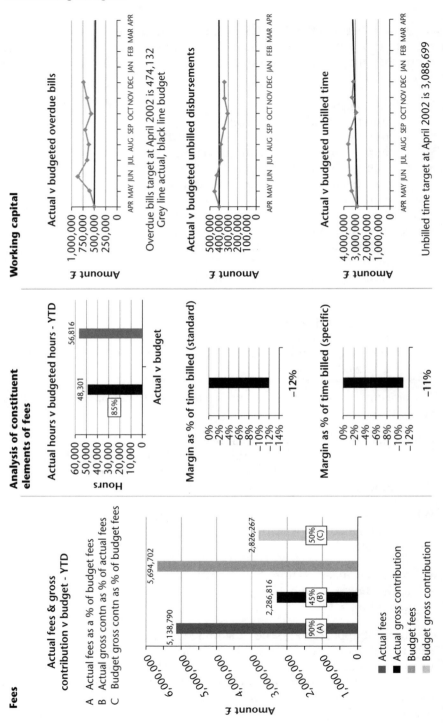

firm Cobbetts in conjunction with their IT supplier Norwel, and uses illustrative figures.

Finance director, James Boyd, uses this report, which is produced on a single sheet of paper, to focus fee earners' attention on the key figures, that is:

- fees and gross contribution;
- hours and recovery;
- working capital.

The report is produced using an Excel spreadsheet, and this automatically changes colour depending on how the actual results compare to budget. Initially it took three or four weeks to produce the scorecard, now it is produced in three or four days.

The Cobbetts' approach is to try to highlight in a simple way the figures fee earners need to action, and enable them to 'drill down', using the information system on their fee-earner desktops, to get at the detail. They also try to focus attention on the exceptions.

CASE STUDY   **Scorecards**

Most of our problems lie with 20 per cent of our fee earners or 20 per cent of our work. We try to concentrate attention on these and let the 80 per cent of straightforward matters proceed as easily as possible. We are particularly keen to help fee earners process transactions smoothly because this helps to control our working capital. For example, we have increased the threshold for manual cheque authorisation from £500 to £5,000 because we found 80 per cent were under £5,000. We use electronic disbursement authorisation for cheques that are under £5,000. We have lightened the controls as far as the fee earners are concerned, but are in fact doing them behind the scenes. We have shifted the role of the accounts department from being a processing unit to one that is more concerned with analysis and checking.

The Cobbetts' scorecard is divided into three sections that look at:

- *the work that has gone out of the door* – in terms of the level of fees and contribution earned;
- *how effective the firm was in doing that work* – by looking at actual versus budgeted hours and the recovery margin (the fee for a piece of work versus the time cost of doing the work);

- *what is left outstanding* – an analysis of working capital – overdue bills, disbursements and unbilled time.

Changing focus

The use of scorecards is a good example of trying to change the focus within a firm so that everyone is looking at the same figures and measures of performance. In the Cobbetts' example, fee earners are likely to be focused on:

- the level of fees their team achieves;
- the profitability of that work;
- time utilisation;
- recovery rates;
- overdue bills;
- unbilled disbursements;
- unbilled time.

Because scorecards are prepared for the firm, each department, each team within the department and each fee earner within each team, it is possible to get everyone focused much more effectively on the same figures.

Such a system is relatively easy for a large firm, but should also be within the grasp of most smaller firms. The scorecard used by Cobbetts uses information imported from their computer system but is actually produced by Excel, a standard Microsoft product all firms will (or should) have. In a smaller firm the figures may have to be manually entered, but there will be fewer of them so it should not be too overwhelming.

SUMMARY

1. The inclusion of work in progress greatly increases the value of a firm's management accounts and makes them much more meaningful.
2. In most cases it will only be practical to prepare accounts that include WIP on a quarterly basis because of the time required to make the figures meaningful.
3. It is possible to improve the focus of fee earners and partners by using concepts such as the scorecard and redesigning the information that partners, department heads, team leaders and fee earners receive, so that they all focus on the same figures.
4. A balanced scorecard can be used to report non-financial information, so providing a more rounded view of the firm's performance.

Improving long-term profitability

11

Developing forward strategy

The starting point in improving the long-term profitability of your firm is to agree its long-term strategy and your overall 'vision' – where you hope the firm will be in five or ten years' time. The second stage is the development of appropriate business and marketing plans to help you get there.

It is quite easy to prepare a business plan, indeed most firms have one. The problem is they are often superficial, prepared for the Legal Services Commission, Investors in People or Lexcel, rather than for the benefit of the firm itself. It is actually quite hard to prepare a good plan, one which everyone 'buys into', and even harder to put it into action.

Arguably, the real benefit of business planning is not the document produced at the end but the process you go through in order to produce it. It is not something to be written by one of the partners over the weekend, so it can be 'ticked off'. If that is how it is done, it will rarely be read by anyone, it will not move the firm forward, and an opportunity will have been missed.

While some firms go through the process, it is very informal – perhaps whilst making coffee each morning, or whilst playing squash or golf. Only some of the partners are involved and it is not written down or necessarily communicated – but they have a plan.

This chapter describes the process firms should work through in preparing a meaningful business plan and Chapter 12 discusses how this should then be translated into a financial projection or budget.

The overall difficulty of planning

Forward planning is often difficult for the following reasons:

- there is too much uncertainty within the firm;
- it can be hard to get fellow partners to take the idea seriously;
- people – especially partners – are too busy, and are not willing to spend what can be a considerable amount of time on something abstract, or something which does not appear to have worked in the past;
- it can be very difficult to look at your own firm objectively – you are too close to it;

- a surprising number of partners have only ever worked at one firm and lack experience of how other firms operate;
- it is more attractive to concentrate on fee earning than to confront potentially difficult decisions about the future of your firm.

Business planning can be a difficult concept to sell to your fellow partners. It can very easily be seen as consultancy gobbledegook and airy-fairy. Seminars on business planning and other management issues invariably attract much lower audiences than those on substantive legal topics. The latter are seen as necessary, the former are not.

The first task, therefore, is to overcome cynicism and get people to take the issue seriously. Perhaps the most powerful argument is that in the long run they will make more money. The most successful firms – those in the upper quartiles discussed in Part II – generally have forward plans and effective management. It is extremely rare that such success happens by chance.

Firms which do not spend time considering the issues are often the ones that experience problems and go into gradual decline. If they do think about the issues it is then too late, their competitors had got there before them. You will know of such firms in your town or county – once good firms that appear to have gradually declined over the years.

Part of the purpose of planning is to generate ideas – many of which won't be taken forward, but some of which will. An equally important objective is to involve people – and thus make it less likely that young salaried partners and assistant solicitors will leave for other firms that are, or are perceived as being, better at involvement and motivation. A well prepared business and marketing plan can make a huge difference to the 'feel' and attitude of a firm. It is a very good way of building a sense of common purpose and is a great tool for coming up with new ideas or solutions to problems.

A good approach to planning is:

- to undertake a comprehensive review of the firm every three to five years – looking at the firm from all angles, and generating an outline plan for the coming three to five years;
- to update this plan annually;
- to monitor progress quarterly and revise the action plan accordingly.

The starting point is the overall review of your firm's operational and management structure discussed in Part I. The people identified in that review should lead the business planning process. The end point should be a very brief document – perhaps just a couple of pages – although behind it may lie weeks or months of work. It is that process – of consultation, both internally and externally, identifying possible options and ideas, and then evaluating them – which is so valuable.

If you wish to achieve long-term change and improvements in profitability, this process of looking in some depth, and fairly objectively, at the business or businesses your firm is in, and how work is processed, has to be the starting point. You should plan over a reasonably long timescale. You are not going to achieve everything in 12 months or change your firm overnight. It is not a quick fix, but one that is quite likely to take several years to achieve.

The three- to five-year review

This is arguably the most useful form of plan – but one that many firms normally skip! Those firms that do undertake such a plan find it helps considerably in shaping the overall direction of their firm, provides focus, and accelerates its development by two or three years. It is a catalyst for change.

In recent years, as business life has moved faster and faster, especially driven by developments in IT, long-term planning has become increasingly unfashionable. Planning periods have shortened from five years to three years, to one year, to six months and even to three months during the dot.com boom. The result has been continuous short-term planning – and a failure to take the longer view and, therefore, the longer-term decisions. Short-term achievement replaces long-term planning and firms become driven by short-term events and opportunities. They can end up moving in unplanned directions. Sometimes these are the right directions but in other cases they can be wrong. The problem is that their development becomes subject to chance rather than being planned.

Undertaken every three to five years, this type of review is an opportunity to take stock and consider the overall direction of the firm for the next few years. You will not be able to predict or plan in detail what will happen but you should be able to identify some of the major trends and set a broad direction.

For example, by 2005/2007:

- It is likely that a significant group of solicitors in England and Wales will be selling property. Solicitors are dominant in most of the cities in Scotland, and at the time of writing, the Scottish model has been introduced into the North East, Yorkshire and the West Midlands. Although still in its infancy, this initiative is likely in the long term to be successful, and gradually the strength and market share of these firms will increase. This diversification will have a big impact on the long-term success of their conveyancing practices.
- It is possible that companies such as Virgin, Tesco or Sainsbury's will be offering legal services. At the time of writing, the RAC has indicated interest in the idea. This could have a huge impact on the high

street and will increase competition for many firms. Others will buy the Virgin franchise for their area and it will be their salvation.

- Alliances with other professions such as accountancy will probably be much more common – and in some cases will be driven by the lawyers rather than the accountants.
- There is likely to be further consolidation in the number of firms undertaking publicly funded work, with a smaller number of firms undertaking legal aid in greater volumes.
- More legal services will be provided over the Internet.

What is a certainty is that the profession will have changed, and there will have been other changes specific to particular areas of work – personal injury, employment, perhaps clinical negligence. Although some of these developments have not happened yet, many of the big issues that will be impacting on firms in 2005/2007 are already here. The value of the three- to five-year review is to try to anticipate what may happen and how your firm should respond. What are the potential opportunities and what are the dangers and threats?

In some instances a specific trigger will prompt the review, such as the retirement of the managing partner, an opportunity to merge with another firm, an abortive merger, looming succession problems, the admission of new partners, declining profitability or simply the recognition that it is some time since the partners sat back and took a longer view of their firm.

Such a review often includes surveys of clients and professional contacts in order to ascertain how the firm is viewed externally. The review will often be led by someone from outside to help the partners look at their firm more objectively, and to drive the process. The review may take some time – often six months or more – and is likely to include a partner or fee earner awayday.

The final outcome should be greater clarity regarding the next three to five years, and normally a big step forward.

CASE STUDY   **One firm's three- to five-year review**

A 20-partner firm concluded a long-term review with a series of meetings for all staff. As each person arrived at the meeting they were given two laminated A4 cards – one summarised the business plan for their team, the other summarised the plan for the whole firm.

The staff were told all the key points. They were told of the partners' overall vision for the firm, the market positioning they were aiming for, and what they hoped the firm would look like in three years' time. They were told about the new office to be opened the following year, the recruitments planned, the anticipated staff relocations and a number of other key points of detail. Everyone directly affected by the changes had already had their views canvassed individually, and each team member had already had an input into at least part of their team plan. Now it was time to explain the plan to all the staff.

The process had started almost nine months previously with confidential surveys of staff, clients and also professional contacts to obtain as wide as possible perspective of the firm. The results of the surveys were summarised and shared with staff. The plan was developed by a steering group of four partners, ranging from the most senior to one of the most junior and the director of finance, assisted by an external consultant.

All the partners – equity and salaried – were involved at half- or full-day partner meetings to update, and receive feedback on the plan as it evolved, and all fee earners contributed to the development of plans for their team.

The result was:

- a plan which everyone had contributed to and most people 'bought into';
- good communications – everyone knew what the plan was;
- action – the firm had made a significant move forward;
- motivation – everyone felt pretty excited!

A suggested content of a business plan – what it should actually look like – is included later in this chapter.

Who should be involved in the planning process?

The business planning process needs to be led by someone – typically the managing partner – and should seek to involve a wide cross-section of people.

In smaller firms all the partners will be involved and other fee earners can be included as appropriate.

Larger firms often find it useful to form a planning committee or steering group to lead and coordinate the exercise. Typically this will comprise the managing partner, key professional managers such as the director of finance or director of marketing and two or three partners drawn from different levels in the partnership. Perhaps a relatively newly appointed salaried partner in their late twenties or early thirties, someone more senior, in the latter part of their career, in their late fifties or early sixties, and someone in-between. This helps to ensure different views are represented. If your firm covers a range of work types or has different offices you may choose to pick people who represent all parts of the firm – but don't make the planning team too large.

Some firms have also included representatives of staff on the working party, and whilst this can be useful it can also severely constrain discussion, and problems can arise when considering confidential issues, especially the accounts, or concerns about particular partners.

When you undertake the three- to five-year review it is good practice in the early stages to involve everyone in the firm by asking them to complete confidential questionnaires designed to ascertain how they think the firm is working. You can learn a considerable amount from such surveys. They must be confidential, however, and go to someone outside the firm. One firm with over 200 staff conducted a survey themselves and had only eight questionnaires returned – all of them critical.

The development of team and departmental business and marketing plans should be led by the management team or team/department leaders, but should involve all the fee earners in the teams because they will know best what is actually happening in the markets they work in.

The way *not* to prepare a plan is for the managing partner or department head to prepare it in isolation without input from their colleagues. In such cases it is their plan, and the firm's other partners and fee earners are likely to happily leave them to implement it.

In one firm, for example, the senior partner took a sabbatical for three months to write the business plan, during which time he rarely appeared! In another firm the plan was about 30 pages long – and most of the action points were to be done by the managing partner, who had written it. He soon became disillusioned because his partners left everything to him.

External surveys of clients and professional contacts

When you prepare a forward business plan it can be especially useful to find out what people outside the firm think of it – and of its competitors.

There are various ways to do this. Perhaps the easiest is simply to ask some of your clients how they feel about the service they are receiving and where it could be improved. A scary question, that takes courage to ask! You could also ask contacts in some of the professional firms you deal with – accountants, surveyors and banks – what they think of your firm and how it compares with others.

The problem with this is they may not tell you what they really think, and you are probably only asking the people who already deal with your firm, and who like it. You also need to ask the people who don't send your firm work. Another problem is that you are probably only speaking to *your* clients – not the clients and contacts of other partners. If you were to get everyone to ask a sample of clients you would have difficulty in collating their responses because they will all ask their questions slightly differently and will interpret the answers in a different way. They will probably only ask their good clients and will avoid the more difficult ones. However, it is at least a starting point and is certainly better than doing nothing.

Some firms have tried to overcome these difficulties by asking all clients to complete a brief questionnaire at the end of each matter – the type of form you might complete when checking out of a hotel. These can be useful, especially as they can apply to all fee earners and can be returned to, say, the marketing department or the managing partner's secretary. After a few months, however, these questionnaires can simply become a chore and lose their value. This type of client survey is probably most useful when it is done for a limited period of time and the results are then compared to earlier periods or across departments.

A variation on this is for the senior or managing partner to telephone a small number of the more important commercial or private clients each month to check everything is going well and that there are no problems. This can work very well and is also an excellent way of building client relations. Partners can easily pick up additional work during such conversations!

The best form of survey is one undertaken by someone independent of the fee earners, such as a marketing assistant, or, even better, someone outside the firm such as a research consultancy. The latter is preferable because some clients are more likely to be open in a questionnaire that is not to be returned to the firm itself. Unhappy clients are the ones you particularly need to hear from.

Typically, a short written questionnaire will be sent to a sample of clients and professional contacts and analysed to provide a snapshot of how the firm is perceived at that point in time. Teams and departments can be compared with each other and over time.

The opinions of professional contacts can be especially useful in assessing how a firm is perceived relative to others. A banker made the following comment:

> There may be a problem that they are too expensive. Probably unjustified – those having the perception almost certainly have no valid comparison. There is a constant need to advertise value for money – if clients want a proper job done in today's legal framework it will cost a realistic amount of money.

Other comments included:

> We perceive them to be strong in all areas with no particular weaknesses.

> In general would appear to be a strong firm.

> . . . being more approachable and getting over the 'too big to care' perception.

> . . . perception of being expensive.

Another firm was once perceptively described as:

> A small boat approaching a large storm with good crew but not sufficient 'craft' to handle it.

Internal surveys of partners, fee earners and staff

It is extremely beneficial to ask staff and fee earners for their views of your firm. Not only is this a good way of making people feel involved, but it can also identify things that need to be changed and generate new ideas. Junior people can often have the most valuable insights into a firm, where it is going wrong and how it could do better. Some examples of their views follow.

What are the best things about the firm?

The service it gives to clients is the best of its kind.
Friendly atmosphere between staff.
Forward thinking.
Loyal, convenient, friendly and those wishing to progress are encouraged.
Having an excellent reputation, being made to feel part of the firm and all working together.
Friendly atmosphere, efficient service.
The friendly atmosphere.
Their commitment to the clients and staff.
Its reputation built over a number of years.

What is the firm not so good at?

Communication at times.
Lack of communication.
Salaries, holiday cover.
Asking everyone's opinion about changes.
Staff incentives.
Possibly a bit outdated with regard to staff benefits, i.e. holiday, pension and pay not particularly up to the level of other firms in the area.
Holding on to good staff, which is more important than a lot of people realise.

The views of trainee solicitors are especially useful because of their experience working in a number of departments. Reception staff also often have a good idea where the problems are!

The key is for staff to feel they are able to answer the questionnaires in confidence and this can be achieved by the questionnaires being analysed by someone outside the firm.

An external facilitator

The key to developing an effective business plan is often the input of someone from outside to help facilitate the process. Many firms use an external facilitator to make the business planning process more meaningful and to overcome the difficulties partners can often have in taking an objective view of their firm.

A facilitator could include the partner who deals with the firm at its accountants, a retired partner of the firm, a management consultant or perhaps a retired local businessman the partners know and respect. There are many good people around, and a good facilitator can turn something bland into something punchy. They can make such a difference for the following reasons:

- Many partners have only ever worked in one firm – they began as a trainee, they qualified with the firm and then became partners.
- Sometimes something has to be said – perhaps about a fellow partner – that would be difficult for a partner to raise. Such issues are better dealt with at an early stage rather than being ignored or allowed to develop into something more difficult to resolve. It is often easier for someone external to raise the issue because they have no agenda, past position, or ulterior motive.
- Junior partners are sometimes reluctant to speak out because this could be taken as criticism and could affect their career prospects. It is safer to talk to an outsider.
- An outsider often sees what the partners – who are too close to the situation – cannot.
- Partners can be unwilling to devote the time needed to develop a well thought through plan. If they are paying someone to help them they are more likely to make the necessary effort.

An external facilitator is particularly useful if you wish to run an awayday or partner weekend as part of the process.

One of the main factors that prevents firms using someone like this is cost. For a very small firm this need not be high, however; two or three hours' consultation for a sole practitioner may only cost a few hundred pounds yet may make a real difference to his or her ideas – a very valuable sounding board. For larger firms a good person should easily be able to justify the cost in terms of the added benefit their input will provide.

Many management consultants are quality assured through membership of bodies such as the Institute of Management Consultancy or the British Accreditation Bureau; alternatively, the Law Society can sometimes point firms towards appropriate consultants.

The overall aims and objectives of the partnership

The first and most important aspect of any business strategy is to establish overall goals for the firm as a whole.

The issues to consider include type of work done (commercial, legal aid, private client); how it is done (highly automated bulk work, or low volume, high value); and where it is done (a single office, through a group of offices, over the Internet). There will be many other questions to consider as well, including the overall size of firm to which you aspire. You may well value your independence and enjoy being involved in decision making. Alternatively, you may recognise that in order to generate the income levels you require, and attract the types of work you do, the firm needs to be larger.

The internal and external surveys discussed above will help inform this process by providing a wider perspective of your firm.

Because of the squeeze on profits in recent years most partners would see increased profitability as a relatively high priority, indeed a necessity in those cases where survival is an issue.

Even firms whose partners have not previously been particularly motivated by money recognise the need to increase profits, otherwise they find it extremely difficult to attract and retain prospective partners.

In Part II we indicated that the most profitable firms had financial profiles along the lines of:

- gross fees per equity partner of around £500,000;
- a gearing of approximately four fee earners in addition to each equity partner;
- a net profit percentage of around 30 per cent (or 15–20 per cent if a notional salary has been included);
- salaries running at 50–55 per cent of fees or less;
- overheads running at around 30 per cent of fees or less.

This type of financial profile will increasingly be included as a target in firms' overall objectives because it is a format that results in higher profits.

What are you, personally, aiming for?

When you have established overall parameters, the second aspect to business planning is an honest appraisal of the personal goals of the key members of the firm.

When a group of people set up a new firm this is discussed at length, but in established firms it is rarely talked about. It is assumed you all want the same; however, this is frequently not the case. It is very important to discuss the variety of ideas and agree what you actually want.

There might be differences between partners according to their age and income requirements. Senior partners with just three or four years to go before retirement may, for example, be reluctant to agree to major investment in new offices or staff. Their profit shares are likely to be reduced by the additional costs and they may well have retired before the expected benefits are seen.

Some younger partners, by contrast, may be very keen to see long-term investment and growth which they see as essential if the firm is to prosper and provide them with a livelihood for the next 25 years or so before they retire. There may be a middle group of partners who recognise the need for long-term investment but need to maximise short-term profitability and drawings because they have mortgages and school fees to pay.

You need, therefore, to be open about what you, personally, want from the firm. This can be surprisingly difficult, especially for lawyers, who invariably hate revealing their 'position'. Years of training as a lawyer seem to fly in the face of the more open approach needed when dealing with fellow partners! Specifically, individual partners need to be willing to disclose:

- how much capital they are able to invest in the firm;
- what levels of profit they require, how much they are able to leave in as capital, and how much they require to draw each month;
- when they plan to retire;
- whether they have any plans to reduce their hours and work on a part-time basis.

Some women partners in small firms have even gone so far as to discuss their maternity hopes and plans, and when they expect to be away from the office on maternity leave. This becomes particularly important where a number of the partners are women who wish to start a family. In one practice four of the five partners were women in their early thirties, and the timings of their pregnancies had a major impact on the firm.

It is especially important to know when partners hope to retire, otherwise succession planning becomes very difficult. Some partners dislike thinking about the issue, and will go to great lengths to avoid serious consideration of their personal retirement plans and their income needs. It can be useful for partners to outline to each other the pension provision they are making, because that can confirm whether or not their retirement plans are realistic.

Having had this discussion, hopefully you will have established that your income needs and the expectations of the firm are similar. This is generally the case. Partners in rural practices, or in particularly attractive locations such as the Lake District, North Yorkshire or East Anglia, often recognise they are willing to accept a lower financial reward because they place a higher priority on their quality of life. This is in part why they became partners in that firm rather than in a city practice. Similarly, partners in commercial firms would normally not question that one of the main reasons for their being there is to earn a very high income.

The problems tend to stem from individual partners who have high income requirements at particular stages in their lives. Sometimes partnerships are willing and able to accommodate this, but in other instances the partner has to resolve the problem themselves. This may mean moving on to another firm that can offer a higher income, finding a way to reduce their expenditure or borrowing personally.

The key is to be realistic about what you are looking for from your firm, and to tell your colleagues.

Agreeing overall strategy and market positioning

Having considered the individual and collective objectives of the partners you should move on to look at the firm's overall market positioning – both now and in the future.

Market positioning is a difficult concept yet it is at the heart of building a successful firm. In essence it is what you want the firm to be known for, by prospective clients and work providers – in effect your reputation. It is a relatively easy concept for niche firms, but more difficult for general practices that have no particular speciality – of which there are many.

An external survey of professional contacts is a very good way of ascertaining how you are currently perceived – and this may well be different from what the partners expect or would like. It is quite common for the perception of external people to be out of date and not to reflect the current position of a firm, owing to the significant time lag between something happening and this being reflected in the firm's reputation in the market. A firm may, for example, develop a capability to undertake commercial work, but it is likely to take some time before people outside the firm – professional contacts – associate the firm with commercial work.

The issue, then, is what you would like your external reputation to be in, say, three to five years' time.

A key strategic objective for many firms is the development of areas of specialisation that will help mark them out from their competitors. After all, it is the features that make your firm different from others that attract clients rather than the features that are similar. It is your specialism in intellectual property or clinical negligence, or the reputation of a particular partner, or the fact that the firm is conveniently located opposite Marks & Spencer that will attract clients.

Hence the need for the firm to be clear as to its areas of strength, and to project this clear message to its market or markets.

This first stage of agreeing a future market positioning can be the most difficult part of the process of developing a forward strategy. With two recent clients I spent four and six months respectively on this single issue, but once it had been decided the rest of the business plan was straightforward!

Examples of firms' intentions include:

To be the leading mental health firm in North London.

To be the principal firm in Hertfordshire.

To be recognised as being the leading firm in our locality for general work, but to have one or two areas – and agriculture is the first – where we are recognised over a much larger geographical area as having expertise on a par with some of the larger firms in Norwich or Ipswich.

One reason why this part can be hard is that it is intangible and rather hard to take seriously, especially for partners who find management as a whole a difficult area. However, it is key to the development of strategy, and is also good fun!

The issue for firms that are currently general practices is whether that is likely to be a successful format in the future. The business planning process in such firms is likely to involve a critical assessment of each area. This may well result in dropping areas that are weak, less profitable or show limited prospects for improvement, and instead developing areas of strength – in effect a move towards being more specialist.

For example, a general high street practice with four partners found it was moving from being a predominantly litigation-based practice to one that had a particularly strong criminal department, operating on a regional and even national basis, whilst continuing a successful local conveyancing business. Because the two markets were different it was perfectly possible to project two quite different messages without causing confusion.

Having agreed an overall target market positioning, you can then move on to prepare a more detailed plan.

What should the plan look like?

The overall aim should be for the plan to be as short and concise as possible. Different types and sizes of firm will need to consider different issues; however, the following headings provide a good general starting point.

Part one: the market and your firm's profile in it

- What is your firm's reputation? How would the firm be described by professional contacts or clients? How does the firm compare with others in your town/city/niche? What is its current market positioning?
- In which areas of law is the firm best? In which areas is it the same as everyone else? Are there any areas in which it is poor?
- What is the mix of work in terms of areas of law and types of client, based, say, on an analysis of fees for the past three years?
- Where does each department's work come from? Are there any particular professional contacts from which you receive a lot of work?
- What is likely to happen over the next three to five years in each of the firm's markets? What will these changes mean for the firm?

Part two: the firm

- How well is the firm managed (in terms of strategic direction and overall management)?
- How good is its administration, its financial and case management systems and its people management?
- What are internal communications like?
- Is good use made of technology? How well are fee earners and staff trained in their use of IT?
- How profitable is the firm and how does it compare to published financial benchmarks?
- Summarise the firm's strengths and weaknesses – and the opportunities and threats facing it (a SWOT analysis).

Part three: overall goal

- What are the individual and collective aspirations of the partners?
- Agree a future market positioning for the firm.
- What would be an attractive goal in five years' time? How far should the firm have got towards this in three years? In one year?

Part four: action plan

- A quarterly action plan for the next year.
- An outline plan for the subsequent two years.
- An IT plan.
- A marketing plan.
- A training plan.
- A budget.

The plan is likely to comprise an overall plan or summary for the firm as a whole and individual plans for each team and department.

Team/departmental plans

Team or departmental plans will be largely based on the headings above. Some topics will not be applicable but most will. There may be additional headings you need to include that are relevant to your firm, for example, a multi-office practice may need to include questions regarding the services to be provided from each office, and communications between the offices.

The overall objective is a realistic assessment of the team's markets and the opportunities and threats facing it. The team would consider its strength and reputation relative to other firms for that work.

You may also try to calculate the total value of the market for the team and its market share. For example, for a client in the Home Counties we estimated the total value of commercial work undertaken by firms in their area to be approximately £4.6 million, with an additional 50–100 per cent being undertaken by London firms, giving a total market of approximately £9 million. We could then work out their market share. For another client, several years ago, we calculated the total size of the legal market in Bridlington at £1.5 million, of which approximately £1.2 million was undertaken by local firms and £0.3 million by firms in Hull.

You can calculate the approximate size of a market by listing all the firms in your area that undertake a particular type of work, say employment law. Then list the actual lawyers undertaking that work in each firm, their names, their ages and a guess as to their likely fees. Use your own fee earners as a yardstick. If your employment partner bills £150,000 a year and an assistant £100,000, take that as your starting point. Because lawyers often know each other and the work they do, it is often possible to make a reasonable guess of someone else's fees. You will know the good lawyers and the poor ones, you will know the people who are efficient and return letters promptly, and often you will know which clients different people act for. You can then calculate the overall size of the market for the work done in your area, make an allowance for work done by firms outside the area, and you then estimate an approximate market share.

Such exercises clearly involve a high degree of guesswork; however, they can help to indicate a firm's strength relative to others.

Team plans need to include input from all the fee earners in a team and should include detailed marketing plans and timetables for areas such as:

- press releases
- articles
- entertaining
- seminars
- corporate events.

Try to avoid having too many action points for each person to do. It is important to be able to review progress and to be able to tick items off. There is nothing worse than an action plan with dozens of points which are never actioned.

Partner awaydays

A partner awayday can be a good way of helping partners to buy into the plan and to contribute in a meaningful way. They are also great ways to allow partners to get to know each other better.

The rules for a successful awayday are as follows:

- Choose somewhere relaxing away from the office. Avoid the temptation of using the boardroom on a Saturday – it does make a difference to get away.
- It is generally not a good idea to use a partner's house unless you are a very small firm.
- Don't invite spouses or partners – this is business and you need everyone's attention.
- Include an overnight stay if possible – it helps team building.
- Involve all partners – equity and salaried – although you may want part of the meeting just for equity partners.
- Make it informal – no suits.
- Consider using an external facilitator.
- Write up the action points immediately – not four weeks later (as in the case of one firm) by which time much momentum will have been lost.

It can be very useful to invite your other fee earners to at least part of the session. They will also find it useful and it is good for them to meet the partners in a relaxed setting away from the office. You may learn a great deal about each other and will see a different side to people's personalities.

Perhaps the most common failure is to expect too much from a partner awayday. They are part of the process of moving a firm forward and you should not have unrealistic expectations of what might be achieved. Perhaps the main benefit is simply that of relaxing and spending time with your fellow partners and getting to know people whom you may otherwise have little to do with. You may meet each month at the partners' meeting but you don't know them. One partner commented:

> I had no idea I had so much in common with him.

Asking difficult questions

If you are preparing a thorough business plan you are likely to begin asking some difficult questions:

- What areas of work should the firm undertake in the future, and what types of clients should it target?
- Are there are any areas of work that are unprofitable, and are likely to continue being unprofitable, that should be dropped?
- Are there any areas that should be developed, and should, for example, the firm move into related fields such as selling property?

Some questions could have a strong bearing on achieving the financial profile of the more successful firms, for example:

- the number of equity partners the firm has now, and how many it should have in the future;
- the competencies required of future equity partners;
- the role of an equity partner and performance expected. The issue of underperformance;
- succession, in particular the increasing difficulty of convincing good people to become equity partners;
- the difficulty in other situations, especially for rural practices, of retaining solicitors if you do not offer them equity.

You should try not to avoid these types of questions. They, and others that will arise, are difficult but important. If you avoid them they are unlikely to go away. They will return the next year, or perhaps the year after, and by then will have become more difficult to resolve. It is often by considering some of the difficult questions that you make progress.

The annual update

The end product of a three- to five-year review should be an overall strategy for the next three to five years and a detailed plan for the coming 12 months. The latter plan needs to be updated annually and the former every three to five years.

The best time to prepare this update is in the final two or three months of the financial year when the outcome for the current year can be seen with some certainty. The new, updated plan should be in place for the start of the new financial year and should link in with the budget-setting process. There should also be a link to the firm's annual appraisal or personal development system.

The format will be similar to the headings outlined earlier in this chapter and the process, too, will be similar, although you are unlikely to undertake external surveys each year.

SUMMARY

1.   The starting point in improving a firm's long-term profitability is to agree its long-term strategy. This is most easily done through the business planning process.

2.   Every three to five years you should undertake a wide-ranging review of your firm and agree a medium-term business strategy.

3.   Update the plan annually and involve all fee earners in the process, especially in the development of team or departmental business and marketing plans.

4.   Use an external facilitator to make the business planning process more effective, and undertake periodic surveys of clients, professional contacts and staff.

Forward financial planning and budgeting

The preparation of an annual budget follows on from the annual update of the business plan discussed in Chapter 11. Budgets are very useful tools for improving long-term profitability because they translate the aspirations and somewhat intangible nature of a business plan into something more specific. The problem is that in many firms preparing the budget is a mechanical exercise in which the opportunity to consider key issues is missed.

Traditionally, budgets have been prepared for 12-month periods, and are used subsequently during the year to compare actual income and expenditure to budget. Whilst essentially this is the correct way to use a budget care must be taken to avoid too much focus on a 12-month period because, as discussed earlier, this can result in too short term a view being taken of the business. Later in this chapter we shall consider the idea of 'rolling budgets'.

Who should prepare the budget, and when?

The best time to prepare a budget is in the final two months of the financial year, when the outcome for the coming year can be seen with some certainty.

The way *not* to prepare a budget is for the finance director or accountant to do it on their own, closeted with a complex Excel spreadsheet! The process needs to be led by your finance staff but must involve heads of department, team leaders and fee earners, especially when considering fee levels and the amount of working capital each team should be working towards.

How should the budget be prepared?

Budgets comprise four elements:

- fees
- salaries
- overheads
- working capital.

Of these four areas, normally it is relatively easy to predict what a firm's overheads and salaries are going to be – whereas setting the fees budget can appear to be the most difficult.

When you are considering the fees budget it is useful to look at past performance – the fees of each fee earner or department or team, perhaps for the past three years. You need to involve the fee earners concerned, they have to feel able to buy into the budget, but it is always best if you can start the discussion with a first draft set of figures – an indication of the level of fees you expect the team to produce.

It is very useful if fee levels can be justified by looking at the hours you expect each person to achieve – both chargeable and non-chargeable – and the hourly rates they typically charge. Table 12.1 illustrates a simple example for a six-partner firm, and the principles would be the same for working out a budget for a department within a firm.

The starting point for this fees budget is the total time you expect each person to be in the office, and the proportion of that time that you expect will be chargeable. I have assumed most fee earners work a seven-hour day, but that partners work 10-hour days. In reality most partners work at least 10-hour days, and this is probably repeated across the professions – most self-employed people tend to work relatively long hours.

I have then made an assumption about the number of chargeable hours each level of fee earner is expected to achieve, and this could be confirmed by looking at the actual chargeable hours your fee earners achieved last year. In this case, five hours a day has been assumed for partners, five and a half for other solicitors and four and a half for the paralegals. Some firms, especially those doing legal aid, would assume higher targets than these and might expect fee earners to achieve six or six and a half chargeable hours a day. You must be very sure such levels are achievable within your own firm before basing a budget on such high levels. It is better to budget for something less ambitious and then beat it, than to be too optimistic in your budgeting.

The average hourly rate could be the fee earner's quoted chargeout rate, or perhaps a better figure to use could be the actual average the fee earner is currently achieving. This is calculated by taking the fee earner's fees – say, for the past three months – and dividing this by the number of chargeable hours recorded. You may then wish to increase the hourly rate to take into account any projected increase in fee rates planned.

This is a good opportunity to review the hourly rates each person charges. It is surprising how many solicitors charge relatively low hourly rates that do not fully take account of their ability or market forces. There is sometimes a reluctance to ask a rate that people feel could be challenged. However, quality is often judged, initially at least, by the rate you quote. To be too low does not help if, in reality, you are one of the leading lawyers in your area for a particular type of work.

Table 12.1 Fees budget

	Total hours per day	Total annual hours	Chargeable hours per day	Annual chargeable hours	Hourly rate £	Total potential fees £	Assume 80% recovery £
Partner 1	10	2,300	5	1,150	140	161,000	128,800
Partner 2	10	2,300	5	1,150	140	161,000	128,800
Partner 3	10	2,300	5	1,150	120	138,000	110,400
Partner 4	10	2,300	5	1,150	120	138,000	110,400
Partner 5	10	2,300	5	1,150	75	86,250	69,000
Partner 6	10	2,300	5	1,150	75	86,250	69,000
Solicitor 1	7	1,610	5½	1,265	110	139,150	111,320
Solicitor 2	7	1,610	5½	1,265	110	139,150	111,320
Solicitor 3	7	1,610	5½	1,265	110	139,150	111,320
Solicitor 4	Assume no fees this year – starts halfway through year						0
Paralegal 1	7	1,610	4½	1,035	70	72,450	57,960
Paralegal 2	7	1,610	4½	1,035	70	72,450	57,960
							1,066,280

As a matter of prudence the totals have then been reduced by 20 per cent. This is a safety margin to allow for a fee earner not achieving either the chargeable hours or the average rate. In particular, fee earners may not always be able to bill all the time recorded on a matter – they do not achieve a 100 per cent recovery – and this makes allowance for this potential shortfall.

This type of analysis is relatively easy where fee earners undertake work that is billed on an hourly basis. It can also be done in many areas of legal aid. If, for example, you know that a fee earner undertakes most of their work on legal aid rates you can calculate their likely fees in the same way. If you undertake claimant personal injury work on a no-win, no-fee basis, you will know what proportion of cases typically are won, and the average hourly rate you are normally paid.

This fees budget straightaway raises a number of issues which should be challenged before the budget is finalised, such as:

* How many hours do you expect each person actually to be in the office?
* How should the partners use their time?
* How many chargeable hours do you expect each fee earner to achieve each day?

The latter in particular requires careful consideration of what each person actually does. It may be, for example, that the paralegals have low chargeable hours because they take on non-chargeable administrative work, especially in the case of some areas of legal aid, freeing others to achieve higher fees.

The fees budget includes a solicitor due to start halfway through the year. This person may, depending on the work they do, generate fees in their first six months, but they may not. In this example a cautious approach has been adopted and it has been assumed they will not generate any fees in this financial year.

The salaries budget, by contrast to the fees budget, is relatively straightforward. The starting point is your current headcount and each person's current salary. You then need to add any additional staff planned for the coming year, and also take account of any expected salary changes. Finally you need to allow for employers' National Insurance Contribution, as illustrated in Table 12.2.

This example includes an allowance for a notional salary for each equity partner. This has been included so as to allow the budget to be assessed against the Law Society benchmarks set out in Part II, but is not essential. If you just want to prepare a straightforward budget that indicates what profit you expect to make this could be excluded.

The final stage in preparing the budget is to consider the firm's overheads. Most people simply take last year's actual and add a percentage to

Table 12.2 Salaries budget

	£
Solicitor 1	45,000
Solicitor 2	35,000
Solicitor 3	28,000
Paralegal 1	18,000
Paralegal 2	16,000
Secretaries (×4)	60,000
	202,000
Pay review: 5% halfway through year	5,000
New solicitor: at £25,000 for six months	12,500
	219,500
NIC (say 12%)	26,300
	245,800
Partners: 6 × £40,000	240,000
	485,800

allow for inflation. This is a useful starting point, but is not the best way. It is far better to work through each line and consider each individually.

Start with the major items – rent and council tax, professional indemnity insurance, depreciation – these three alone will account for a significant proportion of your firm's overheads, and should not take long to work out. With the exception of professional indemnity insurance they are likely to be relatively fixed and you will already know how much to budget.

Of the remaining items, some will apply to the whole firm – such as stationery, telephones, most library expenditure and insurance – but there will be a small number that are specific to particular departments. These will include some marketing (but not firm-wide items such as Yellow Pages), some library (but not the main subscriptions that are firm-wide) and some training. It is a good idea to let each department set a budget for these items and for them to identify their proposed expenditure in these areas. They should prepare schedules itemising what they intend spending their budgets on.

When you are considering the central overheads, it is worth spending time looking at each item and examining where the expenditure went, whether it was required and whether you obtained value for money. One approach is known as 'zero-based budgeting' – which literally means that you start with a budget of zero for each item and then justify each pound spent. Obviously a reasonably broad-brush approach has to be adopted, but this can be a good way of challenging expenditure and obtaining better value. Do not be afraid periodically to put certain areas out to tender, such as insurance, stationery and accountancy and audit. The latter in particular is an area of great variation. Some firms of accountants charge remarkably high fees for a relatively limited, reactive service.

In the case of our example firm, the overall overheads budget was finalised at £297,000 – a reduction of 3 per cent on the previous year. Table 12.3 summarises the overall budget and indicates a projected profit of £283,000. After the partner notional salaries have been added back, this should provide a profit per equity partner of £87,000.

Table 12.3   Overall budget

	%	£'000
Fees	100	1,066
Salaries	46	486
Overheads	28	297
Budgeted net profit	26	283

The percentages in Table 12.3 can then be compared to the benchmarks in Part II to assess how the firm is budgeted to perform – in this case the figures look quite good.

In practice, firms can produce several drafts of the budget before it is agreed, and the process can take several weeks. In industry the whole concept and value of budgeting has been challenged in recent years because of the time required and the limited impact the process can have in large organisations. The process has become an annual chore, especially for the accounts department, rather than something that adds value.

In most professional firms, however, budgets are still a very useful tool because they force partners to think about their income and expenditure, but you should guard against the process becoming routine. It has to add value.

Having completed the profit and loss budget, you will find it very useful to continue the process and set targets for working capital in terms of WIP, disbursements and outstanding debtors. Ideally this should be worked out on a departmental basis, as illustrated in Table 12.4. The starting point is to calculate an amount per fee earner that can then be worked up into an overall target for the department.

It is also useful to set targets for fee earners in terms of chargeable hours – indeed this can often be more useful than a fee target, especially where more than one person works on a file. You might also decide to set targets for non-chargeable time, especially marketing and training.

Twelve-month or rolling?

As discussed at the start of this chapter, budgets are usually prepared for a 12-month period. This is generally very helpful, because the financial year provides a timescale against which progress can be assessed. In many

Table 12.4   Working capital budget

	Target per fee earner (based on historic data for the firm)	£'000
Residential conveyancing (3 fee earners)		
WIP	15,000	45,000
Disbursements	1,500	4,500
Outstanding debtors	5,000	15,000
Family (4 fee earners)		
WIP	25,000	100,000
Disbursements	1,800	7,200
Outstanding debtors	13,000	52,000
Crime (2 fee earners)		
WIP	5,000	10,000
Disbursements	1,800	3,600
Outstanding debtors	5,300	10,600
Commercial (2 fee earners)		
WIP	30,000	60,000
Disbursements	1,300	2,600
Outstanding debtors	19,000	38,000
		348,500

firms one of the biggest problems is getting fee earners to give billing the priority it deserves, and the discipline of annual, quarterly or monthly budgets is an essential stick in this process.

The main problem with this is that fee earners and partners can focus too much on these artificial 'accounting' periods and the year-end can be seen as the all-important deadline – whereas life actually continues afterwards!

It is very useful, therefore, in addition to the normal 12-month budget, to maintain a rolling 12-month forecast that looks further ahead. In effect you are pencilling in another quarter at the end of the budget or the accounts to project current trends further into the future. This only needs to be prepared in outline – a fees figure, salaries and other overheads – possibly built up on a departmental basis, but it means you are better able to project the impact of what is currently happening in the market and to anticipate events earlier.

If your firm prepares accounts on a quarterly basis you would, as part of the accounts pack, include an extra page with an outline projection for the coming nine months – a review of the previous three months plus a projection of the next nine. This will force people to be constantly looking ahead and will make you more aware of trends.

For example, going into a slowdown in the economy, commercial firms may find it more difficult to achieve premium hourly rates, and fee-earner utilisation, in terms of the number of chargeable hours recorded, could fall. Fee earners may also find it hard to achieve their normal chargeout rates and the recovery of the time incurred on matters may become more difficult. A normal budget or set of management accounts will not fully reflect the effect of this, whereas a rolling forecast will.

SUMMARY

1. Budgets are a very effective extension to the business planning process because they translate the aspirations of the plan into something more tangible.
2. The budgets should be led by the accounts department, but certain items, especially fees, need to be agreed at departmental level involving all fee earners.
3. In addition to fee budgets it is very useful to set budgets for chargeable time, WIP, debtors and unbilled disbursements.
4. In addition to a 12-month budget, it is a good idea to maintain a rolling forecast – three months actual plus nine months projected – so as to better assess what will happen in the future.

13

Aligning 'cost' with the fees you can earn

Chapter 12 considered the issue of budgeting and in particular how firms could prepare a fees budget. This chapter looks in more detail at how firms can assess the fees a department or team may earn relative to the cost of doing that work.

In essence, a firm of solicitors makes money when the hourly rate it charges its clients exceeds the cost of that time. If, for example, you are a legal aid firm billing work at rates of, say, £60 an hour, and the cost of your time is £70 an hour you are losing money. If you are able to charge your time at £80 an hour you are making money.

The concept of 'composite cost'

The problem is that it can be very difficult to understand how a team's fees compare to its costs because of the range of hourly rates that can be paid – especially with regard to legally aided work.

One way of overcoming this is to assess the cost of your firm's time by calculating a 'composite cost' for all the fee earners in the firm. In effect, you take the total salary and overhead costs of your firm and divide this by the total number of hours available to give a blended or composite cost.

The easiest way is probably to take your firm's latest management accounts or the budget for the coming year. The illustration in Table 13.1 is in respect of this firm's budget for the year to 31 March 2003.

The salaries budget is £1,108,000 and overheads amount to £767,000. This firm is based outside London and a notional salary of £40,000 has been used for each of the seven equity partners. An allowance has also been made for a pension provision for the equity partners – of 17.5 per cent – and also for interest on partner capital. In this case it is assumed each partner has capital of £80,000, and interest has been assumed at 6 per cent.[1]

This provides a total 'cost' for the firm of £2,237,600. If this is billed the partners will receive their notional salary, pension provision and interest on capital account, but no profit in excess of the £40,000 salary.

It is in effect a 'zero profit' calculation and merely reflects the cost base of the firm.

In all, the firm has 25 fee earners – comprising eight solicitors, two trainees and eight other fee earners in addition to the equity partners. You need to decide how many hours each person is likely to work.

In its 1992 edition of the booklet, *The Expense of Time*, (now out of print), the Law Society assumed fee earners would achieve 1,100 hours per year. The Law Society of Scotland, in its booklet, *The Cost of Time*, assumes 1,000 hours a year for equity partners and trainee solicitors and 1,200 for all other fee earners. It has made an allowance for the management workload a partner has and has also acknowledged that a trainee will not achieve the same hours as a qualified solicitor.

Table 13.2 broadly follows the Scottish model, except a more prudent 600 hours has been assumed for trainees. An alternative could be to take the average of each fee earner's actual chargeable hours over, say, the past three years. The difficulty of this is that few firms have sufficiently reliable time recording that is consistent across the firm, and that those that do often find that whilst some fee earners achieve very high chargeable hours others can be lower. It is often easiest to agree a middle course and

Table 13.1   Composite cost illustration, year to 31 March 2003 – the cost base of the firm

	£
Staff costs	1,108,000
Overheads	767,000
Equity partner notional (7 × £40,000)	280,000
Allowance for equity partner pension (£280,000 × 17.5%)	49,000
Allowance for interest on partner capital (7 × £80,000 × 6%)	33,600
	2,237,600

Table 13.2   Composite cost illustration, year to 31 March 2003 – available hours

	Number	*Standard hours*	*% time fee earning*	*Total hours*
Managing partner	1	1,000	50	500
Other equity partners	6	1,000	100	6,000
Salaried partners	0	1,200	100	0
Associate or assistants	8	1,200	100	9,600
Trainees	2	600	100	1,200
Other fee earners	8	1,200	100	9,600
				26,900
Composite cost £2,237,600/26,900				**83.18**

apply that to everyone. There is a particular danger in assuming very high chargeable hours as these may not be sustainable in the long term.

Table 13.2 indicates that this firm has a 'capacity' of 26,900 hours a year (or just over 500 hours a week). If this is divided into the total cost base of £2,237,600, the firm's composite is found to be £83.18.

It should be noted that 'cost' is before any credit for interest earned on the basis that such income is dependent on prevailing interest rates and also the amount held on client account, which can vary. Figure 13.1 illustrates the actual composite cost for the 5–10 partner firms outside London in the LMS survey[2] and illustrates that most firms achieved a composite cost of approximately £60–£80 an hour, lower than the firm illustrated.

Figures 13.2 and 13.3 illustrate the results for the smaller 2–4 partner firms and the larger 11–25 partner firms. All three figures are for firms outside London as relatively few London firms participated in the survey.

Most firms should find it interesting to calculate their own composite cost. If your figure is high relative to the LMS survey, does that make sense? Would you expect your cost base to be high? If you wouldn't, you might find it useful to look into your salary and overhead costs more carefully and try to identify areas where you may be out of line compared to other firms of your size in your locality.

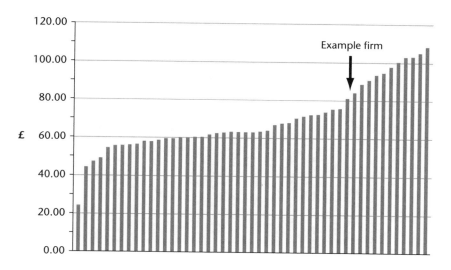

Figure 13.1   Composite cost, 5–10 partners – LMS
Source: BDO Stoy Hayward/LMS Financial Benchmarking Survey 2001

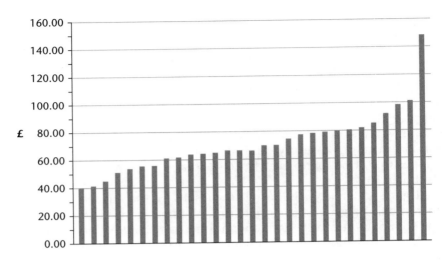

Figure 13.2 Composite cost, 2–4 partners – LMS
Source: BDO Stoy Hayward/LMS Financial Benchmarking Survey 2001

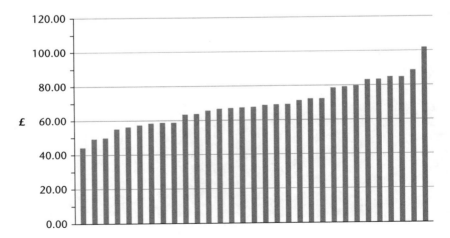

Figure 13.3 Composite cost, 11–25 partners – LMS
Source: BDO Stoy Hayward/LMS Financial Benchmarking Survey 2001

Average hourly profit

It is useful then to go on and compare your firm's composite cost to its average hourly fee.

The firm illustrated had a total fee income of £2,400,000 and therefore achieved an average fee per hour of £89.22 (£2,400,000 / 26,900). They therefore made an average hourly profit of £6.04. This is quite good, as illustrated in Figure 13.4 which provides the average hourly profit for other firms of its size from the LMS survey.

As discussed above, any interest earned on client account has been excluded from this calculation, and a notional salary has been included for each partner; however, where a firm is making a 'loss', this may mean that the partners' actual profit shares are below the notional salary. Figure 13.4 indicates a wide spread with almost half the firms making an hourly loss – of up to £10 an hour – and just over half making a profit.

Figure 13.5 illustrates the average profit per hour achieved by the 2–4 partner firms in the survey and indicates a similar pattern.

Figure 13.6 indicates that most of the 11–25 partner firms are at least breaking even, with some earning as much as £40 an hour. This difference between the smaller and larger firms may well reflect the different proportions of their work accounted for by legal aid and residential conveyancing.

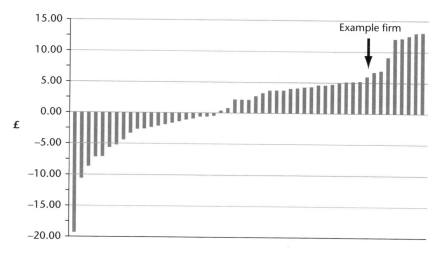

Figure 13.4   Average hourly profit, 5–10 partners
Source: BDO Stoy Hayward/LMS Financial Benchmarking Survey 2001

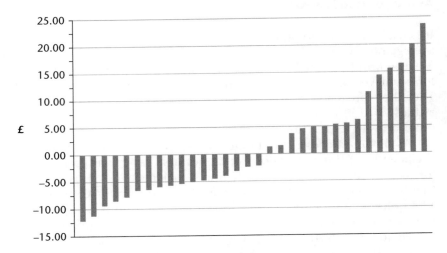

Figure 13.5 Average hourly profit, 2–4 partners
Source: BDO Stoy Hayward/LMS Financial Benchmarking Survey 2001

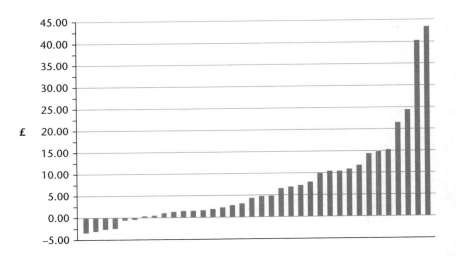

Figure 13.6 Average hourly profit, 11–25 partners
Source: BDO Stoy Hayward/LMS Financial Benchmarking Survey 2001

Having calculated an overall average hourly profit for your firm, you may well find it informative to calculate an average for each department or team. The composite cost is likely to be the same across the firm, but the average hourly fee could vary considerably. This is calculated by taking the fees for each team and dividing this by the capacity of that team, as illustrated in Table 13.3.

The departmental average hourly fee is a key figure that many firms monitor each month or quarter, as illustrated in Table 13.4. It is the end product of a number of factors, including the quality of work undertaken and the efficiency with which that work is done.

In this example, the average for each department is monitored quarterly in respect of that quarter. An alternative would be to calculate a rolling average for the past 12 months. By the end of September 2002 three departments – Family, Probate and Personal injury – had already beat the budgeted levels although Residential conveyancing was still below. This had been expected to be the most difficult area but the partners

Table 13.3 Composite cost illustration, year to 31st March 2003 – average hourly profit, departmental analysis

(£)	Residential conveyancing	Family	Probate	Personal injury	Total
Managing partner	500				500
Other equity partners (6)	1,000	2,000	2,000	1,000	6,000
Associates or assistants (8)	2,400	2,400	2,400	2,400	9,600
Trainees (2)		600	600		1,200
Other fee earners (8)	1,200	3,600	2,400	2,400	9,600
Departmental capacity	**5,100**	**8,600**	**7,400**	**5,800**	**26,900**
Fees	318,750	750,000	739,650	591,600	2,400,000
Average hourly fee	**62.50**	**87.21**	**99.93**	**102.00**	**89.22**
Average hourly cost	83.18	83.18	83.18	83.18	83.18
Average hourly profit/(loss)	**−20.68**	**4.03**	**16.75**	**18.82**	**6.04**

Table 13.4 Composite cost illustration, year to 31 March 2003 – average hourly fee, quarterly monitoring

(£)	December 2001	March 2002	June 2002	September 2002	December 2002	March 2002	Budget
			Actual, for each quarter, as at September 2002				
Residential conveyancing	56.25	57.85	55.29	60.54			62.50
Family	85.25	86.45	87.02	89.54			87.21
Probate	99.95	98.78	101.25	102.85			99.93
Personal injury	99.25	101.25	104.52	106.54			102.00

in that department are optimistic they will hit the budgeted rate by the end of the year.

Variation in composite cost

A firm's composite cost is clearly going to be influenced by a number of factors. Some of the most important are:

- the fee-earning capacity of a firm in terms of the number of fee earners it has and the hours they work. Where firms have a small number of fee earners the fixed costs of the firm have to be recovered by a smaller number of people. Where there are more fee earners and greater capacity the fixed costs can be recovered more easily;
- the level of a firm's cost base – some firms operate from low cost offices and are very cost conscious in all areas of expenditure. Others spend money much more freely;
- the type of work undertaken – in particular, firms that undertake a significant amount of crime tend to achieve a lower average cost because they have fewer secretaries;
- a firm's gearing. Firms with a high proportion of non-partner fee earners tend to achieve low average costs.

The latter point has a significant impact on cost and is illustrated in Figure 13.7. This indicates that firms where more than 75 per cent of the fee earners were not equity partners achieved a composite cost 25 per cent less than firms where only 50 per cent were not equity partners.

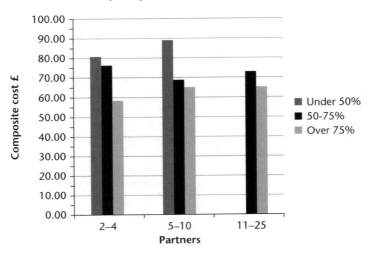

Figure 13.7 Composite cost – by percentage of fee earners who are not equity partners
Source: BDO Stoy Hayward/LMS Financial Benchmarking Survey 2001

The principal elements of composite cost

Table 13.5 provides an analysis of the composition of cost. It indicates that around half the hourly cost comprises staff costs, and this rises to nearly two-thirds if equity partner notional salaries are included. Of the remainder, accommodation costs account for around 7 per cent, IT, marketing and training around 6 per cent, equity partner pension and interest around 3 per cent, and 'all other expenditure' around 20–24 per cent. This will include professional indemnity insurance, which typically accounts for another 5–7 per cent, and a wide range of other expenses including telephone, postage, light and heat, library, accountancy, bank interest and charges, etc.

Curiously, there is often little difference between firms of these sizes in London and in the provinces. Although rents in the City and the West End of London are high, there is often little difference between the rents paid elsewhere in London and a provincial legal centre. For example, in many towns and cities the solicitors tend to be based in very small areas, often close to the courts, where rents can be quite high – in Sheffield, the area around Paradise Square, in Watford on Station Road. Rents can be as high for the Sheffield or Watford firms based in these areas as they are in many of the London boroughs, where firms often have a much wider choice of location.

Table 13.5 Analysis of average composite cost

Percentage	2–4 partners	5–10 partners	11–25 partners	Overall
Fee earners	24	26	31	28
Secretarial/other departmental staff	13	14	13	14
Non-departmental staff	8	9	9	9
Total staff	**45**	**49**	**53**	**51**
Equity partner notional salaries	14	12	10	12
Total including notional salaries	**59**	**61**	**63**	**63**
Accommodation	7	7	8	7
IT	3	3	3	3
Marketing	1	2	2	2
Training	1	1	1	1
Equity partner pension provision	3	2	2	2
Interest on capital accounts	2	1	1	1
All other expenditure	24	23	20	21
	100	100	100	100

SUMMARY

1. As an extension to the annual budget, you should also calculate your firm's 'composite cost'.
2. You should also calculate the average fee for the firm and for each department.
3. Assess the resulting figures and see whether they make sense – this will help your understanding of the profitability of the various areas of work.
4. Monitor average fees on a monthly or quarterly basis and use this to try to improve the profitability of each area of work.

Notes

1   The 17.5 per cent pension and 6 per cent interest provision are based on the figures used in the Law Society of Scotland's annual cost of time calculation.
2   This analysis of composite cost was undertaken after the 2001 report was published, but a similar analysis is likely to be included in the 2002 survey.

14

Implementing the plan and managing change

Implementing the plan

Preparing a business plan and budget is the (relatively) easy bit – implementing it is more difficult!

The key is to make the action plan as short as possible, break it down into quarters and then review progress every three months. You might decide that in your firm you are going to monitor progress monthly, which is fine, but it should not be longer than three monthly. Three months is a good time period because it is long enough to get things done, but not so long that they are forgotten!

One of the dangers of preparing a business plan, especially if you conclude the process by going on a partner weekend, is that you finish up with dozens of action points – many of which won't get done. For example, one firm came away from a partner retreat with about 45 action points. A year later they looked back and concluded that about a third had been ditched within a month – although they had seemed a good idea at the time, back in the reality of the office they made less sense. About a third had been implemented, whilst the remaining third, including some of the most important, had really not moved forward. The result was a feeling of failure and disillusionment with the process. Two or three partners had invested a great deal of time and effort in the weekend, and they especially felt let down.

It is better to come up with a relatively short list of important action points, ideally broken down by team, that actually get carried out. This induces a more positive climate in which partners feel they are making progress and you can then move forward and develop the plan with more confidence.

Ideally, each team should meet monthly to review progress, and every three months both to review progress, and also revise the action plan for the coming quarter. In this way the plan becomes a living, rolling document that is constantly reviewed and revised. The annual updates become much easier because people are familiar with the plan, know how they are doing and will already be thinking about the next phase.

Responsibility for implementation lies with the team leaders who should report progress to their head of department or the managing partner – on a monthly or perhaps quarterly basis. Prior to meeting with the managing partner the team leaders could produce a short report that could be copied to team members, although care would have to be taken in discussing staffing or any confidential issues if such a document is going to be made more widely available.

Each quarter's progress against budget can also be monitored and, once again, it is good to let all fee earners in a team have a copy of the team's financial position, perhaps using one of the formats discussed in Part II.

To reiterate, every month you should review progress against the action plan and every quarter review progress, review performance and update both the action plan and budget as appropriate.

Getting people to change

Lawyers are accustomed to change – the law is constantly changing and developing – it is a fact of life. An additional factor in recent years has been that the environment in which lawyers work has also changed – in many cases out of all recognition – and that can be extremely hard to cope with. Much management time is devoted to the management of change, and it is not easy.

In particular, most people dislike change and find it difficult to deal with, especially if they are faced with change on all fronts. It can be intimidating and it also requires the one thing most fee earners lack – time.

Most people in the early part of their careers don't have major problems with adjusting to change. They may object vehemently to changes that affect their day-to-day lives such as a new secretary, or new office, but they are normally able to adjust to change much more easily than colleagues in their fifties and sixties – although there are some notable exceptions. Some firms have senior partners who put their younger colleagues to shame with their willingness to embrace new technology and change in general.

There are two main groups of people who are often resistant to change:

- some (but not all) more senior partners, especially those with heavy fee loads, who can be reluctant to adopt new working methods;
- some (but not all) more senior secretaries (often those who work with the partners who are resistant to change). These people have often been with the firm for years, they are really only there for the salary and have a very nine-to-five attitude. Such people can be a particular obstacle, and it is remarkable the impact that just one or two of them can have.

These two groups of people can be a considerable barrier to change and can cause endless frustration to other partners and members of staff.

There are, perhaps, three or four main areas with which people have difficulty that can impact on a firm's ability to implement their business plans.

1. Keeping up with changes in the law and in the marketplace

Good examples of changes in the marketplace would be both defendant and claimant insurance work. Many firms that used to do defendant work have suffered sudden falls in work levels as insurance companies have cut their panels. Similarly, many that undertook claimant work have seen traditional sources of personal injury cases dry up over a period of time and go instead to 'claims farms'. These companies have then passed the work on to the firms on their panels, but the profitability of the work is greatly reduced.

Partners and other fee earners in these firms, who had not really had to worry where their next client was coming from for 20 or more years of their careers, can find it bewildering suddenly having to think about marketing and having to identify new sources of work. It can be very hard to start thinking about such issues when you are 55 – and all the people in the insurance companies appear to be in their thirties!

2. Adapting to new working methods

It is remarkable how many people still claim to have a fear of using computers and new technology at work when most have computers at home and are quite happy using the Internet to keep in touch with friends and family. There are some genuine and well founded concerns about the tendency to cut secretarial support to fee earners but many people lack imagination in thinking about new technology and how they could use it in their work.

A greater difficulty is, arguably, the changes in how a case is actually progressed – dictated by changes in court practice, funding methods or client demands. The shift from legal aid to conditional fees, for example, required a major change in thinking which many found very difficult, and which some fee earners, used to years of working in a legally aided environment, simply could not adjust to.

3. A reluctance to change because of high caseloads

Many fee earners – especially partners – can appear unenthusiastic to change, whereas the real problem lies in their workloads. In many firms there is intense competition amongst partners to achieve high personal fees, and this is especially so in those firms that place too much emphasis on individual fee targets. In some cases this is imposed from above, in others fee earners have a natural desire to compete with each other. The result can be fee earners with extremely high caseloads.

This has been a particular problem with both residential property and legal aid lawyers in recent years. As conveyancing fees have fallen, the response has been to take on increased numbers of cases in order to achieve the same level of fees. This has resulted in caseloads which require long hours and cause excessive stress. Legal aid lawyers have increased their caseloads and hours worked over several years of very low, or no, pay increases.

The last thing someone struggling with a very high caseload needs is for additional jobs or apparently unnecessary changes to their work.

4. Slowing down with age

Some partners are able to work and bill at the same levels when in their fififties and sixties as they did in their thirties and forties – but many are not. Also, senior partners invariably spend more of their time on the management of their firm and on tutoring/mentoring younger colleagues. Many firms still set individual fee targets and do not make allowance for these factors, instead giving all partners the same targets. The result can be that these more senior partners feel under immense pressure to achieve the same levels of fees as their younger colleagues. Because they are more senior and often deal with more complex cases, they believe they should achieve high fee levels and are surprised when they struggle. The result can be that they work ever longer hours and start hanging on to work they should delegate. Their younger colleagues perceive them as stubborn and reluctant to change.

A by-product of the difficulty in managing change is that the management burden often falls on just a few people – sometimes some of the highest billing partners. They know that if they don't try to manage the firm, no one else will. These people embrace change but because they are already very busy they finish up with an even greater workload as they try to combine fee earning with management.

A common theme underlying all of these issues is that partners and fee earners are increasingly struggling to cope with growing volumes of cases without changing their working methods. They have too many cases and too little support – many fee earners still work in isolation, just with a secretary. And in London, in many smaller firms, increasingly they don't even have a secretary. Competition from the City has meant that many smaller firms have great difficulty matching salaries, and increasingly fee earners become self-supporting, with all the implications that can have on productivity.

The result is fee earners who have very little time for anything other than fee earning and who, over time, can become demoralised. Rather than taking on more cases and working longer hours, you will find that a better solution is to be more selective in the work you take on, to put more thought into the level of fee earner who should do the work, and to think more seriously about whether you can be smarter in your working methods.

In many cases part of the solution is to move away from the traditional fee earner/secretary structure and towards better team working, with a partner or solicitor working in a small team with a paralegal, and probably a secretary. Paralegals are invaluable people as they can do the routine aspects of the case and free up the fee earner to concentrate on the more complex tasks. This works well in many areas, but especially so in crime, residential conveyancing, personal injury and to some extent family. By working with a paralegal/secretary as a small unit, and provided everyone is properly supervised, the fee earner is able to deal with a higher volume of cases much more efficiently and has more time as a result. It is a way of overcoming the problem of lack of time, and helps make the job of fee earner more enjoyable.

This concept of a fee-earning unit – a fee earner, paralegal and secretary – is even more important when the fee earner has a significant management role. Such support is particularly important in small firms, where the partner often takes on a management workload in addition to a full caseload. An untenable long-term situation.

So, in helping people to change, a good starting point is to try to understand better the work and working methods of individual fee earners, the problems they face, and the things they enjoy. The most effective method of doing this in a structured way is via an appraisal or personal development process.

Individual action plans, personal development plans and appraisals

The perennial problem for team leaders is to get people, especially fellow partners, to do what they have said they will do especially when they are busy with casework, and in particular when they have never really bought into the process in the first place.

One way to overcome this problem is to link the team business plans into individual action plans – or 'personal business plans' – and the firm's appraisal system.

Just as many firms have business plans but don't derive full benefit from the process, many firms have appraisal systems, but don't really use them properly. Frequently firms recognise that the appraisal system should be a very useful tool, but seem to have great difficulty in making it work for them.

The problem stems in part from their view of what the appraisals are actually for, in part from a lack of training, and in part through poor design of the procedure and forms. Neither does the name help, and some firms have stopped using the word 'appraisals', instead calling them 'personal development reviews'.

Some firms still view appraisals as part of their disciplinary system rather than as a tool for developing and getting the most from their people. Their real role is the latter. If you have a disciplinary problem with someone the appraisal interview is unlikely to be the place to deal with it. It should have been dealt with already. If you are to use appraisals as a tool to get the most from your people you need to:

- ensure they apply to everyone – including the equity partners;
- put some time into designing an effective system;
- give some thought as to who is going to conduct the appraisals;
- train those people.

By linking a firm's business and marketing plan with what you expect from each person via the firm's personal development or appraisal process, you will find that it is possible to make much faster progress than might otherwise be the case.

An interesting approach to this is illustrated in the following case study from Jeffries Solicitors in Essex.

CASE STUDY   **Performance management**

If we are to manage our people effectively in a demanding business environment, traditional appraisal methods will invariably fall short of the mark. Management style has to be empowering, communicative, motivating but also honest, providing clarity so staff know what is expected of them. This is achievable through Performance Management techniques, which adopt a coaching style rather than the historic 'telling' approach to appraisal.

Performance Management (PM) involves the agreement of standards and targets for each tier of staff reflecting the overall objectives of the firm in any financial year. Thus staff have clarity regarding what is required at the start of the year rather than a retrospective review at the end of the period. Performance plans would typically cover such areas as financial results, team working, client satisfaction and business growth depending on the role undertaken.

Once agreed, the performance standards become the focus of a quarterly, two-way discussion to identify areas of performance that are going well and those that require some attention. Using the coaching approach (ask not tell), actions are agreed for each party to undertake to ensure that, say, fee earner and secretary work more effectively together going forward. Indeed it is essential that staff are 'performance managed' by their immediate line manager to ensure that a close working relationship is developed for mutual benefit and ultimately the firm's gain. It is the quality of the quarterly debate, conducted in a constructive, open but honest manner, which makes PM such a powerful management tool.

The final part of the process is a fourth and final quarterly review at the firm's financial year-end at which a performance rating is agreed to reflect achievement against the individual's and ultimately the firm's objectives. Personal ratings could be 'Exceed', 'Succeed', 'Developing' or 'Fall Short' which then introduces performance to the bigger issue of deciding pay and reward. PM has proved to be simple, effective and above all, attractive to staff given its constructive approach compared with previous more dictatorial methods of assessment.

By linking your firm's appraisal system closely with your business planning process you should find it easier to obtain commitment and achieve the gradual change in attitudes required in order to achieve long-term improvements to profitability.

It is essential that the appraisal process includes the partners. In many firms appraisals stop as soon as someone becomes a salaried partner, yet often partners have the most to benefit, especially when they have been a partner for several years. The problem can be making appraisals real and meaningful, especially when you have been in partnership with someone for a long time. The answer is to use some imagination in how the appraisal system is designed.

For example, one firm in Cambridgeshire decided that all the partner appraisals would be undertaken by one of the salaried partners – someone everyone respected and who would do the job well. Another firm in Manchester decided that each equity partner would have an interview with another equity partner together with a salaried partner. The key is to be imaginative and to identify the best way of gaining real benefit from the process.

You should also ensure the process is not just one way – it is not just you appraising your secretary. It should include an opportunity for the person being appraised to give constructive feedback to the person conducting the appraisal on how they can improve their performance.

These meetings, handled in a constructive way, can provide an invaluable forum to discuss someone's role in the firm and their future career development. The key is to listen, to be constructive and to be willing to discuss issues openly.

Personality profiling and psychometric testing as a tool in identifying potential

One way of becoming more sophisticated at identifying the strengths of your people is to use psychometric testing and measurement.

This area has grown rapidly in the past 20 years or so and there are now hundreds of commercially available tests and questionnaires which are used widely to assess the differences between people. Psychometric tools can be used in both a development and a selection context. They can be extremely useful when recruiting new solicitors, especially prospective partners, as they are a good way of getting behind the 'gloss' people put on at interview. They are also a good way of understanding better the skills each person has and can help in planning a person's career development. They can be used to provide insight and a benchmark against which to differentiate between individuals.

Most UK companies now use psychometric measures in some way or another.

Psychometric tests have right or wrong answers and are used to measure an individual's specific aptitudes or abilities. Included within this category would be tests to measure verbal, numerical and problem-solving ability.

Psychometric questionnaires do not have right or wrong answers. They give an indication of personality, preferences, values and relationships with others. They provide a profile of the candidate's perception of their behaviour at work. By understanding an individual's style, you can gain information on how they will fit in within certain work environments and teams and how they will cope with different job requirements. These instruments give significant and accurate insights when completed honestly, but are not infallible.

Psychometric information should only be used with the guidance of practitioners who are familiar with its value and limitations and who have qualified at least to Level B of the British Psychological Society's arrangements for test users.

One of the partners in a firm in South Yorkshire decided to try a personality test himself so as to better understand how it could be used in his firm:

I approached personality profiling with some scepticism, but agreed to try profiling of myself to form an assessment of its usefulness. I was surprised and impressed by the detailed, in-depth analysis and the way in which this was done. By approaching a number of areas from different angles, a detailed picture of strengths, weaknesses and character traits was constructed, on the basis of a detailed questionnaire that I completed.

I certainly felt that this could be of tremendous value in recruitment, both as to the general character of applicants and as to whether the particular strengths and abilities required for a certain area or type of work are identified.

The key is once again to be imaginative in using established management tools and techniques, and there is a wide range of human resource related ideas such as this that many firms would find beneficial.

Changing attitudes

Much of the effort of improving long-term profitability involves changing the attitudes of partners, fee earners and staff. Changing attitude can be difficult and takes time. It involves a recognition of the need to change, willingness on the part of those affected and an atmosphere of trust.

Attitudes a firm may wish to change could include:

- the tendency to take on work regardless of its profitability and whether the firm is going to be paid;
- the assumption that a fee earner's value is measured primarily by the fees they bill;
- a lack of willingness to pass work on to others more suitable to do it;
- reluctance and difficulty in cross-selling each other's services.

It is often difficult to get partners and fee earners to face up to many of these issues because figures turn them off and they don't have time for administration. It can be difficult to get their attention. Also, the climate of fee-based assessment makes it appear threatening to challenge attitudes.

An important first stage is to get their commitment, and the business planning and budgeting process described in Chapters 11 and 12 can help achieve this. This should be led by and supported by the managing partner and other key partners in the firm. The appraisal or personal development processes described in this chapter can also have an important role in changing attitudes because they provide an ongoing opportunity to reinforce the need to change.

A large part of the trust within a partnership is determined by the attitude and the style of the senior and managing partners; however, it is possible to ease partner fear and insecurity by dealing with a number of 'structural' issues regarding the partnership. These include:

- having a partnership agreement – it is surprising how many firms do not have one;
- including a retirement age in the partnership agreement – increasingly firms are opting for something under 65, in some cases 60;
- agreeing job descriptions that define the role of each equity partner;
- agreeing a basis of sharing profits that includes an element related to performance and also a 'tailing off' in shares in the last few years towards retirement;
- agreeing a 'partner protocol' dealing with respect towards each other, and also with the firm's staff.

Change, especially at partner level, can often involve alterations to the work a person does, the development of new areas, and the passing on of existing areas of work to colleagues. The invariable result of change is that partners see their individual fee levels fall, at least in the short term.

This is not a problem in well run firms, but in many practices partners are preoccupied with their own personal fee levels and see them as the key measure of their worth and contribution to the partnership. The result is that partners are unwilling to do anything that could adversely impact on their own personal fee levels. Their concern often flows from the issue of profit allocation and their belief that they will lose out personally if their fees fall.

It can be very hard to change these attitudes in a firm because they can be very deeply held; however, firms that are too preoccupied with individual partner fee levels tend, in the long run, to be less profitable than those that are more focused on team performance. Firms have tried to overcome these problems in a variety of ways. Some practices that do not work on an equal or 'lockstep' basis (see below) have tried to broaden the criteria upon which profit allocation is based by introducing a wider range of other factors, such as:

- overall profitability of team;
- level of working capital reduction for the team;
- amount of new business acquired for other teams;
- overall contribution to marketing;
- contribution to the training and development of other fee earners;
- contribution to overall management.

Most firms allocate profits either equally or according to lockstep – the process whereby partners build up a full equity share over a period of five to seven years, which they keep until retirement. These two methods have the great advantages of being simple and providing certainty, but they have the drawback that they fail to recognise exceptional performance. They can also fuel resentment towards partners who, for a variety of reasons, are underperforming. A better way is to allow an element of the profits – perhaps 5 per cent – to be allocated on a performance basis. It will be necessary to agree a basis for assessment, and normally it is best to get someone external, such as your accountants, to draw up the rules.

One way of helping to ease partners towards retirement, and of taking pressure off them in their last four or five years is to introduce a system of 'reverse lockstep'. This is a staged reduction in profit shares in the final three or five years leading up to retirement – perhaps back from 100 per cent to 50 per cent. This frees up profits to bring in a junior partner and can take the heat away from partners who still have much to contribute but who have difficulty, at the age of, say, 62, performing at the same level as when they were 42.

This can also help deal with the workaholic partners who are still working ridiculous hours, including weekends, in their early sixties. The knowledge that their profit shares are reducing each year can be a powerful force in getting them to slow down – and probably thereby living much longer and more happily after retirement.

The reason many partners keep working longer than they would ideally like is that they have not made adequate pension provision during their careers. Whilst you may not wish to incorporate a requirement into your partnership agreement, firms should make every effort to ensure their partners, especially their younger ones, make adequate provision. The incorporation of a retirement age into a partnership agreement helps because it provides certainty and assists with succession planning. It helps avoid the prospect of partners continuing well after they should have retired.

Respect

Respect, not just for the senior partner but for fellow partners and staff, is another powerful tool in creating an environment in which partners feel sufficiently safe and confident to change and adapt.

Traditionally, many partners have been poor at showing respect and sometimes even courtesy towards their staff (and their fellow partners) – and some still are. Once again, there is a real difference in the 'feel' of firms where the partners have addressed the issue and those that are better at this are likely to be more successful in the long term. They will have better working relationships and people will feel more willing to move into new or embryonic areas of work. They are less likely to feel their jobs are at risk.

The key to this is the recognition that each firm member plays a valuable role, and not simply as a fee generator or income earner. In assessing each person, partners should give proper weight to management issues and other forms of contribution to the success of the firm. If, on honest assessment, a fee earner is found not to be contributing in a global sense, then this should be addressed in the person's appraisal interview or it should be recognised that they do not have a long-term future with the firm. The key to the assessment, however, is a recognition that a good contribution to the management of the firm counts as essential 'work'.

Some firms have agreed a partner/staff protocol that all partners have signed. This can be a useful tool in making it more difficult for partners to obstruct management. The protocol might include an agreement to:

- respect each other;
- share responsibility;
- criticise ideas not people;
- keep an open mind;
- attend all meetings;
- listen constructively;
- keep promises.

Sometimes the protocol is in the form of a small statement that is put on noticeboards and distributed to all staff – once again making it more difficult for partners to go back on the principles.

Another way of encouraging partners to change and adapt is to offer protected profit shares for a period after the change. For example, in larger firms where the managing partner role is full time, candidates for the position are offered a protected full profit share for two or three years on returning to fee earning to enable them to rebuild their legal practices.

Motivating staff

It is very much easier to implement a business plan and to manage the process of change if everyone – fellow partners and staff – is motivated. The problem is that many firms are still very poor at motivation. They might have good IT systems and case management but people management and motivation is still in its infancy in many firms.

A particular problem is the assumption on the part of many partners that most people are primarily motivated by money.

Firms that conduct exit interviews[1] often find that salary is not the main reason for a person leaving. There are often other factors that are more important, as illustrated in Figures 14.1 and 14.2.

These two figures are based on a brief questionnaire completed by a small number of staff[2] – secretaries and assistant solicitors drawn from firms mainly in London and the South East. They were asked to select the five most important factors in their personal motivation from a list of 10 possibilities. The figures indicate that whilst salary was one of the most important factors there were others – and these are the factors often overlooked by firms.

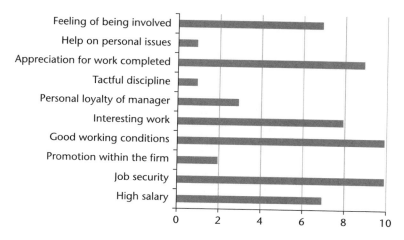

Figure 14.1 What motivates people? A young secretary

Amongst the secretaries the top factors were job security, good working conditions, appreciation for work completed and interesting work – followed by high salary and a feeling of being involved. The reason for job security being so important may have been that one of the 'magic circle' London firms had just announced a round of secretarial redundancies, and there was also the general uncertainty caused by the move in many firms towards self-supporting fee earners.

Amongst the assistant solicitors, having a high salary came top together with interesting work, followed by promotion within the firm, good working conditions and a feeling of being involved.

The mistake many firms make is to place too much emphasis on money and neglect the other factors. Some compound the problem by introducing bonus schemes – often highly complex and related to personal fee targets – to motivate people. Yet such schemes often have the effect of undermining many of the goals in the firm's business plan. If they are not properly controlled they can encourage fee earners to hold on to cases they should have passed on to others, perhaps more junior or in other departments, they often undermine team working and do nothing to motivate support staff. A better solution is a bonus related to the profitability of a team, shared amongst all the members of the team – fee earners and secretaries – together with a bonus for central staff related to the overall profitability of the firm.

In order to be successful you have to have good people. This means paying good salaries and offering a good overall package. It also means:

- showing appreciation for work completed – in particular encouraging your partners and other fee earners to say 'thank you' more often –

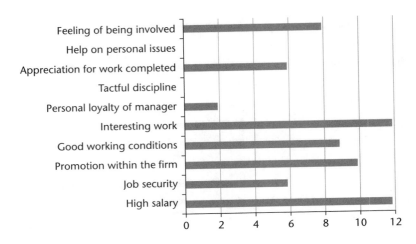

Figure 14.2   What motivates people? – A young assistant solicitor

something many lawyers, especially when under pressure, are poor at. It costs the firm nothing yet does wonders for motivation!

- helping people to feel involved by sharing information – especially financial – and involving them in team or firm-wide meetings;
- thinking more carefully about who should do what, with a view to giving more people work that is interesting. Whilst all firms will have much work that is relatively boring and repetitive there is also much that is interesting, especially for the junior people and support staff. If you are able to give more people tasks that they enjoy and consider important, they will feel more motivated and will give the firm more in return;
- being willing to discuss promotion prospects in an open way. The annual appraisal interview is normally an appropriate time for this. As discussed earlier, the key to profitability in many firms is the number of equity partners relative to other fee earners and fees, and the result is that many solicitors who might have expected equity partnership will not get it. But they may well become salaried partners and you may be able to offer them an overall package and feeling of self-respect that means they stay with your firm. But it has to be discussed;
- providing your staff, especially your support staff, with good working conditions. This may mean reasonably new furniture, a reliable computer, flexible working or air-conditioned offices. In many cases the starting point is to ask them;
- making it very clear that fee earning is not the only issue – team enhancement, good use of IT, good relations with fellow staff and clients, and ultimately a contribution to management, are all very important.

SUMMARY

1. Monitor the action plan quarterly in teams and review and update on an ongoing basis.
2. Invest time with individual people to understand better the pressures on them and their personal barriers to implementing the plan and to change.
3. Use the appraisal or personal development system to develop individual action points.
4. Try to instil a culture of respect and security, especially amongst the partner team, as this makes it easier for people to change.
5. Remember that money is only one of the factors that motivates people – and in many cases it is not the most important.

Notes

1   An exit interview is a structured interview with a member of staff before they leave the firm to learn more about their reasons for leaving and their views of the firm.

2   As part of the pre-course preparation for 'Law firm management – for new/prospective partners and associates', Girton College, Cambridge, June 2002.

15

Conclusion

Success in a law firm today requires more than good legal skills – you need to develop good business skills and strong management awareness. This book has tried to tackle the main problem areas facing firms with a view to helping partners identify the questions they need to be asking. The answers will be different for each firm – the starting point is to ask the right questions!

> To successfully manage and develop a small or medium-sized law firm, just being a good lawyer or great fee earner is not enough. The leaders of a modern law firm must embrace the best management practices and be prepared to inform and challenge themselves. If firms are to maximise their potential and maintain their competitive edge in a rapidly changing professional and social environment, they must adapt.

You should not feel daunted by tackling these issues and should always remember that good management can simply lie in clear solutions. You should also allow a reasonable timescale – you will not change your firm overnight but steady progress is essential.

The key areas to remember are:

* focus and agreement on the long-term goals for your firm;
* implementing an appropriate management structure;
* identifying the best people to fill this management structure;
* steadily developing team and firm-wide business and marketing plans;
* establishing strong and effective financial management;
* providing a consistently high standard of client service;
* finding ways of motivating your partners and staff.

> I had previously been uncertain what questions to ask, had not known what data to gather in order to extrapolate the answers, and had lacked the confidence to implement the conclusions. I now understand what we are supposed to do and that my hunches had been correct. We are now much more confident in how we should move forward.

Appendix A

The Lexcel Practice Management Standards

The Lexcel Practice Management Standards (PMS) were revised in July 2000.

Lexcel's Practice Management Standards provide a guideline against which practices can measure the way they currently manage themselves as well as a checklist for planning improvements and developments.

The Legal Services Commission has incorporated many of these standards as part of the requirements for their own quality mark (LAFQAS/CLSQM), so any practice which already has LAFQAS/CLSQM is also likely to have met many of the requirements of the PMS in those areas.

The standards do not prescribe procedures and systems in detail. Instead, they identify the key disciplines in which procedures and systems are needed that will suit the needs of both the practice and their clients. Sources of precedents and further guidance are suggested below.

Compliance with the Solicitors' Practice Rules, etc.

All solicitors are subject to the general law, the Solicitors' Practice Rules, Solicitors' Accounts Rules, Investment Business Rules, and the other requirements in *The Guide to the Professional Conduct of Solicitors 1999*. These requirements are not repeated in these standards. However, establishing systems and procedures as suggested by the standards will assist practices in ensuring compliance.

In order to achieve Lexcel:

- **practices must comply with all the core Practice Management Standards which are indicated by the words 'will' and 'must' and the use of bold type;**
- **the word 'should' indicates a recommendation;**
- **the word 'may' conveys discretion.**

A: MANAGEMENT STRUCTURE

A1 **Practices will have a written description of their management structure which designates the responsibilities of individuals and lines of accountability. There will be a named supervisor for each area of work (a supervisor may be responsible for more than one area). The** supervisor must have appropriate experience of the work supervised and be able to guide and assist others.

A1.1 The management structure should be appropriate for the partners, principals, and staff, the size of the practice, its location, and the type of work it does.

A1.2 Practices should be able to explain their management structure, for example to incoming partners, principals or staff, and the written description may for example:

a) List the designated responsibilities of individuals in the practice (including responsibility for adherence to these Standards)
b) Name committees (if any) and summarise their terms of reference
c) Describe reporting structures in the practice, for example by including a 'family tree'.

A1.3 Supervisors should be able to describe their experience and the ways in which they guide and assist those under their supervision.

B: SERVICES AND FORWARD PLANNING

B1 Practices will document:

a) Key objectives for 12 months and an outline strategy covering a further two years to provide a background against which the practice may review its performance and may take decisions about its future. Plans must identify the resources and skills necessary to deliver the strategy, with a finance plan and budget. Plans must include an information technology strategy
b) The services they wish to offer; the client groups to be served; how services are to be provided; and the way in which services are designed to meet client needs
c) Their approach to marketing
d) Reviews of all elements specified in B1 at least every six months.

Practices may choose the format and level of detail of documentation that suits them best.

B1.1 This documentation need not be disclosed to third parties.

Strategy

B1.2 The strategy should be sufficient to provide a framework for decisions about, for example, capital expenditure (including computers), office location, staffing, strategic and business risks facing the practice, changes in the external environment and targeting new business, but need not be written in considerable detail.

B1.3 Most practices will already have agreed annual budgets, financial targets, etc. (as well as views about how the practice ought to develop) and these provide a useful starting point for strategy planning. A finance plan may consist of a projected profit and loss account in detail for one year and in outline for the subsequent two years.

B1.4 Practices may wish to consider the following:

a) Setting goals for the practice for the coming five years
b) Adopting a 'practice purpose statement' describing the long-term aims of the practice.

Services

B1.5 How the practice provides services will depend upon its clients and services. Issues may include location of offices, physical access to the premises, languages spoken, facilities for clients, electronic communication, etc. These issues should normally be addressed in the practice's strategy.

Marketing

B1.6 A marketing plan should form part of the practice's strategy. For those satisfied with their current quality and level of business, a marketing plan will need to be less detailed than for a practice wishing to expand, develop a new specialism, or uncertain about its future client base. For some areas of work, the plan may need to describe how to contain demand to an acceptable level (rather than how to encourage additional business), taking account of that work's profitability and the resources of the practice.

B1.7 A marketing plan may:

a) Describe the services to be provided and client groups to be served, how services will be delivered, and the practice's client care policy
b) Describe the practice's resources including skills and knowledge
c) Set out objectives for the clients or business to be developed, which should be measurable and related to a timeframe
d) Explain how the structure or personnel or organisation of the practice will need to develop if those objectives are to be attained
e) Provide a timetable for marketing activities and a budget
f) Allocate and describe appropriate individual responsibility for the marketing activities
g) Describe arrangements for monitoring response to the marketing effort (for example recording sources of referrals, etc.).

Non-discrimination

B2 Practices will document procedures on non-discrimination, and have regard to guidance on non-discrimination in accepting instructions from clients and the provision of services issued by the Law Society from time to time.

See also D8.

C: FINANCIAL MANAGEMENT

Responsibility

C1 Practices will document responsibility for financial affairs.

Financial information

C2 Practices will be able to provide documentary evidence of the following:

a) Annual budget (including, where appropriate, any capital expenditure proposed)
b) Quarterly variance analysis of income and expenditure against budget
c) Annual profit and loss account
d) Annual balance sheet
e) Annual cash flow forecast
f) Quarterly variance analysis of cash flow.

C2.1 In addition, practices may find it helpful to maintain the following management information (but note that it will not be practicable to produce much of this in the absence of full computerisation):

a) Separate capital expenditure budget
b) Weekly or monthly aged list of debtors
c) Analysis of the cost of services (including apportioned overheads)
d) Analysis of cases by category
e) Analysis of cases by client name
f) Analysis of fees by fee earner
g) Analysis of fees by category or department
h) Analysis of working capital.

C2.2 Note that practices will not normally disclose financial information to third parties; but, for example, they may in appropriate cases instead make available an accountant's certificate that systems to provide the relevant information within the practice itself are in place.

Computerisation

C2.3 Implementation of a computerised accounting system will assist cost-effectiveness. It is unlikely that most practices could comply with these Standards in the absence of computerisation. Practices will note that B1a requires an information technology strategy.

C2.4 Computerised accounting systems can maintain financial records as required by the Solicitors Accounts Rules and provide other reports and information as well. Details are given in the Law Society's directory publication: *The Software Solutions Annual Guide.*

C2.5 There is a significant cost in money and time attached to planning for development of information technology, including purchase of software, training and support following implementation. But, if properly planned, this investment will be worthwhile.

Time recording

C3 **Practices will have a documented system that ensures that time spent on casework can be properly recorded and attributed.**

C3.1 The system may provide that some matters or types of matter need not be subject to time recording (for example, where a fixed fee has been agreed) and in that case time recording should be carried out on a sample basis.

D: MANAGING PEOPLE

Job descriptions

D1 **Practices will document the skills, knowledge and experience required of fee earners and other staff, the tasks they are required to perform, usually in the form of a written job description; but employment contracts may reserve job flexibility.**

D1.1 Practices may prepare a personnel plan to help ensure that skills, knowledge and experience within the practice are developed to meet needs indicated in the forward planning documents (section B).

Recruitment

D2 **Practices will have documented arrangements which evaluate the skills, knowledge and experience possessed by applicants for posts in the practice, and their integrity and suitability.**

D2.1 For example, applicants may be sent a copy of the job description and a form to complete; and the contents of completed applications may then be checked against the requirements in the job description; and questions at interviews may be related to the completed application and to the job description.

New post-holders

D3   Practices will have documented arrangements to provide an induction process for new post-holders.

Objectives and performance appraisal

D4   Practices will have documented procedures to:

a) Record the responsibilities and objectives of each partner, principal, and member of staff in the practice
b) Evaluate performance of staff at least annually against those responsibilities and objectives
c) Record in writing the performance appraisal, the record to be kept confidential to the practice and to the post-holder.

Training

D5   Practices will have documented arrangements to ensure that:

a) All partners, principals, and staff are trained to a level of competence appropriate to their work
b) Training and development needs are assessed for each person against the objectives of the practice and are reviewed at least annually
c) Skills and knowledge required for the management and organisation of the practice (as well as for legal practice) are provided for in training and development
d) Appropriate written training records are maintained.

D5.1 Practices should also ensure that for cost-effectiveness and to maximise development of the practice's own resources, skills and knowledge acquired by fee earners and other staff are communicated within the practice through training in-house.

Communications

D6   Practices will have documented arrangements (informal or otherwise) which foster communication within the practice, and encourage suggestions for improvement.

Supervision

D7 Practices will ensure that there are appropriate documented arrangements for supervision (supervision of casework is the subject of F10).

Equal opportunity

D8 Practices will document procedures on equality of opportunity including recruitment and employment procedures and have regard to guidance on equality of opportunity issued by the Law Society from time to time.

See also B2.

E: OFFICE ADMINISTRATION

Responsibilities

E1 Practices will document the facilities needed to provide services including:

a) Maintenance and support services
b) Health and safety conditions
c) Annual review of risk.

E1.1 Issues addressed in the review of risk in relation to facilities should include health and safety considerations.

Forms and procedures

E2 Practices will maintain an Office Manual collating information on office practice, which must be available to all members of the practice. There will be documented procedures to:

a) Note each page with the date and/or number of issue
b) Review the Manual at least annually
c) Update the Manual and record the dates of amendments.

E2.1 Precedents for office forms and procedures are offered in the Law Society's *Lexcel Office Procedures Manual*.

Legal reference material

E3 Practices will have documented arrangements to ensure that:

a) Fee earners have ready access to up-to-date legal reference material for the areas in which the practice offers a service

b) Fee earners receive timely information about changes in the law, practice and procedure relevant to their work.

F: CASE MANAGEMENT

Systems

F1   Practices will have documented arrangements to:

a) Maintain an index of matters
b) Facilitate identifying any conflict of interest
c) Monitor the number and type of matters undertaken by each fee earner to ensure that they are within his or her capacity
d) Maintain a back-up record of key dates in matters
e) Ensure proper authorisation and monitoring of undertakings given on behalf of the practice
f) Ensure proper risk management procedures are in place, including:
   i.   Appointing an overall Risk Manager for the practice
   ii.   Maintaining information about the generic risks associated with the type(s) of work carried out
   iii. Listing and defining types of case which are likely to fall within acceptable risk levels
   iv.   Listing and defining types of case which are likely to fall outside acceptable risk levels
   v.   Implementing procedures to manage all cases which fall outside acceptable risk levels, including mitigating actions and contingency plans, where appropriate
   vi.   Conducting an annual documented review of all risk assessment data generated within the practice.

F2   Where required to do so by a third party funding the legal costs of a matter, or by a client instructing the practice in a number of matters, the practice will have a system which enables all relevant matters to be identified.

Client care

F3   Practices will have written procedures to ensure compliance with the Solicitors Costs Information and Client Care Code 1999 and to provide for clear and regular communication with clients, third parties and the court as necessary in relation to costs.

They must:
a) Inform clients of the basis of charging
b) Provide the client with advance costs information including:
   i.   The best information possible about the likely cost, including a breakdown between fees, VAT and disbursements
   ii.   Where time spent is a factor in the calculation of the fees, a

        clear explanation of the time likely to be spent in dealing with the matter

  iii. Agreeing a fixed fee; or giving a realistic estimate; or giving a forecast within a possible range of costs

  iv. Informing the client if any estimate or quotation is not intended to be fixed, and if charging rates may be increased

  v. Explaining to a private paying client that the client may set an upper limit on the firm's costs, which may be reached without further authority

  vi. Explaining to the client the reasonably foreseeable payments which may be required to be paid to the solicitor or to a third party, and when those payments may be needed

  vii. Arrangements for updating costs information and informing the client at regular intervals (at least every six months)

  viii. Whether the client may be eligible for any public funding, and if so, the costs implications for the client, particularly in relation to the statutory charge, where applicable

  ix. Whether the client's liability for costs may be covered by insurance or another party, e.g. a Trades Union

  x. Whether the client's liability for another party's costs may be covered by insurance.

F3.1 Practices may use standardised checklists to ensure appropriate information is obtained and given at each stage of a matter.

At the outset of a case

F4   Practices will establish a documented procedure for taking instructions which will ensure that fee earners:

a) Agree and record:
  i. The client's instructions and objectives
  ii. A clear explanation of issues raised and the advice given
  iii. Action to be taken by the practice and likely timescale
  iv. Strategy decided upon and any case plan
  v. The name and status of the person dealing with the matter and the name of the person responsible for its overall supervision and whom to contact about any problem with the service provided

b) Confirm these with the client (ordinarily in writing)

c) Provide written information to the client about complaints procedures

d) Identify key dates in the matter and record these in the file and in the back-up system

e) Discuss with the client whether the likely outcome will justify the expense or risk involved, including, if relevant, the risk of having to bear an opponent's costs

f) Consider whether there is any unusual degree of risk to the practice associated with the matter and record this on the office file

g) Implement procedures to manage risk to the practice assessed at unacceptable levels in accordance with the practice's documented procedures.

Progress of the matter

F5   Practices will have documented procedures to ensure that:

a) Information on progress of the matter (or reasons for lack of progress) is given to the client at appropriate intervals
b) Information about changes in the action planned to be taken in the matter, strategy or case plan, its handling (including person with conduct), or cost, is given to the client promptly
c) The client is informed in writing of any circumstances which will or may affect the degree of risk involved or cost benefit to the client of continuing with the matter
d) A timely response is made to correspondence and telephone calls
e) Information on cost, and in publicly funded cases, the effect of the statutory charge if any, is given to the client in writing at least every six months and timely reference is made to the client when an agreed limit on costs or stage in progress is approached
f) In litigation matters information about adverse costs orders is given to the client immediately as payment may be required forthwith
g) A case plan may also be prepared in a complex matter, agreed with the client, and periodically reviewed and updated.

Documents, etc.

F6   Practices will have documented procedures to ensure that they are able to identify and trace all documents, correspondence and other information relating to a matter and that these are properly stored and are readily accessible.

At the end of the case

F7   Practices will have documented procedures to ensure that at the conclusion of the matter, the practice:

a) Reports to the client on the outcome and explains any further action that the client is required to take in the matter and what (if anything) the practice will do
b) Accounts to the client for any outstanding money
c) Returns to the client original documents and other property belonging to the client if required (save for items which are by agreement to be stored by the practice)
d) If appropriate, advises the client about arrangements for stor-

age and retrieval of papers and other items retained (in so far as this had not been dealt with already, for example in terms of business)

e) Advises the client whether they should review the matter in future, and if so, when

f) Carries out a concluding risk assessment in relation to the case

g) Notifies the practice's overall Risk Manager if the final assessment differs from the initial assessment, and provides a written explanation.

Services from others

F8 Practices will establish a documented procedure for using barristers, expert witnesses, etc. in providing the practice's legal services which will include provision for the following:

a) Use of clear selection criteria which should not discriminate in relation to gender, sexual orientation, race, disability or religion

b) Where appropriate, consultation with the client in relation to selection, and proper advice to the client on choice of advocate

c) Maintenance of records (centrally, by department, or by office) on barristers and experts used

d) Giving of instructions which clearly describe what is required and which, in litigation matters, comply with the rules of court and any court orders

e) Checking of opinions and reports received to ensure they adequately provide the information sought (and, in litigation matters, comply with the rules of court and any court orders)

f) Payment of fees.

File management

F9 Practices will have documented arrangements to ensure that:

a) The status of the matter and action taken can be easily checked by other members of the practice

b) Documents are arranged in the file in an orderly way

c) Key information is shown clearly on the file (for example at the front of the file) which will include details of any undertakings given on behalf of the practice.

File review

F10 Practices will have documented arrangements to supervise the conduct of casework, and these will include:

a) Availability of a supervisor to guide and assist others

b) Appropriate procedures to allocate work in relation to the qualifications and experience of fee earners and their workloads

c) Arrangements for the management of case files to be reviewed periodically and the review will (except where there is only one fee earner in the practice) be carried out by a fee earner who has not been involved in the day-to-day conduct of the matter

d) A record of the review to be kept on the case file and on a central record

e) Arrangements to ensure that any corrective action identified is carried out promptly.

F10.1 It will be a matter for each practice to determine the frequency of such reviews and whether all files are reviewed or a sample selected.

F10.2 Practices may also adopt other arrangements to ensure appropriate supervision of casework. Options include:

a) Checking incoming post

b) Outgoing post signed by supervisor

c) Regular review sessions with a supervisor, covering:
   i. New cases taken on, and discussion of 'case plans' in complex cases
   ii. Progress review for current cases
   iii. Evaluation of outcomes of completed cases
   iv. Consideration of training needs in relation to legal knowledge and skills.

Complaints

F11 Practices will have documented arrangements for complaints handling, including:

a) Definition of a complaint

b) Making the complaints procedure accessible to all clients, and providing a copy of the complaints procedure on request

c) Reporting and recording centrally every complaint made by a client

d) Responding appropriately to any complaint within a defined timetable

e) Identifying the cause of any problem of which a client has complained, offering any appropriate redress, and correcting any unsatisfactory procedures

f) An annual documented review of any complaints to establish issues where client care may be improved, including clients' perceptions of the procedure itself.

Appendix B

The Lexcel Self-Assessment Checklist

The Lexcel Self-Assessment Checklist is a useful audit tool for you to establish how much of the Lexcel standard your practice already has in place.

Your practice is likely to be meeting a number of the Lexcel requirements already (especially if you have other quality standards in place, in particular LAFQAS/CLSQM). Before proceeding with Lexcel, practices will therefore find it useful to complete the Checklist, and correct any identified weaknesses prior to assessment.

It may be necessary to repeat the self-assessment process a number of times before arriving at a satisfactory result. A practice should therefore make as many copies of the Self-Assessment Checklist as necessary.

LEXCEL CERTIFICATION
SELF-ASSESSMENT CHECKLIST

PRACTICE DETAILS

NAME:
ADDRESS:

TELEPHONE & FAX:

ASSESSMENT CONTACT:

CHECKLIST HEADINGS

There are four headings contained in the Checklist form:

Standard
This sets out the reference number of the relevant Practice Management Standard.

Mandatory Requirement
This summarises, very succinctly, what the Standard requires.

How Complied With
This should be completed with a brief description of the relevant procedures and supporting documentation that exists within the practice.

Document Reference
You should use this column to indicate where to find relevant documentation in your practice. If individual documents are referred to, the practice should index them sequentially, for example, document A, document B, etc.

N.B. A practice should make as many copies of the self-assessment checklist as needed, always keeping a blank to be completed when the self-assessment process produces an entirely satisfactory result.

Standard	Mandatory Requirement	How Complied With	Doc. Ref. OM = Office Manual
A – Management Structure			
A1	Documented management structure		
	A named supervisor for each area of work		
B – Services and Forward Planning			
B1	Review at least every 6 months:		
	a) Documented outline strategy for the practice		
	b) Documented services plan		
	c) Documented approach to marketing		
B2	Documented equal opportunities policy in respect of the provision of services		
C – Financial Management			
C1	Documented arrangements to demonstrate who is responsible for financial affairs		
C2	Demonstrate existence of financial information:		
	a) Annual budget		
	b) Quarterly variance of income and expenditure		
	c) Annual profit & loss account		
	d) Annual balance sheet		
	e) Annual cash flow forecast		
	f) Quarterly analysis of cash flow		
C3	Documented system for time recording		
D – Managing People			
D1	Documented skills, knowledge, experience required of, and tasks to be performed by fee earners and other staff in the practice		

Standard	Mandatory Requirement	How Complied With	Doc. Ref. OM = Office Manual
D – Managing People (continued)			
D2	Documented recruitment arrangements to evaluate skills, knowledge, experience, integrity and suitability of applicants		
D3	Documented arrangements for induction		
D4	a) Documented responsibilities and objectives of partners, principals/members of staff		
	b) Documented arrangements to evaluate performance of staff at least annually		
	c) Documented record of appraisals		
D5	a) Documented arrangements to ensure partners, principals and staff are properly trained		
	b) Documented arrangements for review of training and development		
	c) Documented arrangements for management training		
	d) Training records		
D6	Documented arrangements to foster good communication		
D7	Documented arrangements for (non-casework) supervision		
D8	A documented equal opportunities policy in respect of the treatment of staff		
E – Office Administration			
E1	Documented facilities needed to provide services		
	a) Maintenance & support services		
	b) Health & safety conditions		
	c) Annual review of risk		

Standard	Mandatory Requirement	How Complied With	Doc. Ref. OM = Office Manual

E – Office Administration (continued)

E2 Office Manual available to all
- a) Pages dated/issue numbered
- b) Reviewed annually
- c) Updated & records kept

E3 Documented arrangements to ensure that:
- a) Fee earners have access to up-to-date legal reference material
- b) Fee earners receive information on changes in the law

F – Case Management

F1 Arrangements to:
- a) Maintain an index of matters
- b) Identify conflict of interest
- c) Monitor workloads
- d) Maintain a back-up record of key dates
- e) Ensure proper authorisation and monitoring of undertakings
- f) i. Risk Manager
  - ii. Information on generic risk
  - iii. Listing cases within acceptable risk levels
  - iv. Listing cases outside acceptable risk levels
  - v. Risk management procedures
  - vi. Documented annual review of risk

F2 Documented system identifying all matters for a client or funder if required

Standard	Mandatory Requirement	How Complied With	Doc. Ref. OM = Office Manual

F – Case Management (continued)

F3 Documented procedures to comply with Practice Rule 15/ Solicitors Costs Information & Client Care Code 1999

F4 Documented procedures for taking and following up instructions including:

a) Agreeing and recording:
  i. Client's instructions
  ii. Issues raised and advice given
  iii. Action to be taken
  iv. Terms of business
  v. Name & status of the person with conduct/overall supervisor/ complaints contact

b) Confirming the above with the client

c) Providing written information on complaints procedures

d) Identifying and recording key dates in the file and the back-up system

e) Discuss with client if outcome justifies risk of costs, etc.

f) Consider risk to practice

g) Manage risk if unacceptable

F5 During the matter, documented policies which ensure:

a) Information on progress (or lack of it) is given to the client at appropriate times

b) Information on changes in the action planned, its handling and cost are given promptly

Standard	Mandatory Requirement	How Complied With	Doc. Ref. OM = Office Manual

F – Case Management (continued)

F5
c) Client informed of circumstances affecting risk of continuing with matter

d) Timely response to letters/telephone calls

e) Information on cost/statutory charge every 6 months or when an agreed limit or stage is approached

f) Information on adverse costs orders provided to client immediately

F6 Documented procedure for identification of all documents and other information relating to a matter, files stored properly & accessibly

F7 At conclusion of the matter, documented procedures to:

a) Report to the client on the outcome

b) Account to the client for any outstanding money

c) Return any original documentation

d) Advise the client about storage and retrieval of papers and other items

e) Advise the client whether and when to review the matter

f) Carry out concluding risk assessment

g) Notify Risk Manager if final assessment differs from initial assessment

F8 Procedure to advise, select barristers and expert witnesses including:

a) Use of clear selection criteria

b) Consultation with the client

c) Maintenance of central record of barristers and expert witnesses used

d) Giving clear instructions to barristers and expert witnesses which comply with rules of court

Standard	Mandatory Requirement	How Complied With	Doc. Ref. OM = Office Manual
F – Case Management (continued)			
F8	e) Checking adequacy of reports and opinions		
	f) Payment of fees		
F9	Documented arrangements to ensure that:		
	a) Status of the matter may be easily checked		
	b) Documents are arranged in an orderly way		
	c) Key information is clearly shown on the file, including details of any undertakings given		
F10	Documented arrangements for supervision of casework:		
	a) Availability of supervisor		
	b) Work allocated as appropriate		
	c) Review of management of files		
	d) Record of review on file & central record		
	e) Corrective action carried out promptly		
F11	Documented arrangements for complaints handling:		
	a) Definition of a complaint		
	b) Making the procedure accessible		
	c) Reporting and recording every complaint		
	d) Responding to timetable		
	e) Identifying the cause & correcting defective procedures		
	f) Annual documented review of complaints		

Further reading

Mowbray, Robert (1997) *Maximising the Profitability of Law Firms* (Blackstone).

Otterburn, Andrew (1998) *Cashflow and Improved Financial Management* (The Law Society).

Otterburn, Andrew (1998) *Profitability and Financial Management* (The Law Society).

Porter, David S. and Openshaw, Vanessa (2001) *Business Management for Solicitors* (Emis Professional Publishing).

Walden, Julia (1999) *Credit Management for Law Firms* (CLT Professional Publishing Limited).

Westwood, Fiona (2000) *Achieving Best Practice* (McGraw-Hill).

Index